ESSENCE

ENDING EMPTINESS, FINDING FULFILLMENT

APRIL ADAMS

ISBN-13: 978-1505347494
ISBN-10: 1505347491
Library of Congress Control Number: 2014921738
CreateSpace Independent Publishing Platform, North Charleston, SC.

This book is dedicated to all of my fellow seekers. May you find your bliss.

TABLE OF CONTENTS

Introduction

Disclaimer

The ideas and methods in this book are sourced from my own intuition, experience and research. Please take what resonates with you and leave the rest. There are concepts that I state as fact, and while they are true for me, they may not be your truth. I resonate strongly with non-traditional beliefs, as they make the most sense to me on a soul level. I encourage you to open your mind & your heart to discovering your own truth. Follow your inner guidance as to what you choose to live and believe. I would never ask anyone to blindly believe anything. I am simply sharing what has worked for me. All I ask is that you try my suggestions out and see what works for you.

If you are new to metaphysical and spiritual concepts, or are a non-believer, all I ask is that you go into this book with the mindset of "What if this is possible? What can it hurt to try it?" When I began my journey, I would treat every book I felt guided to read as my Bible for the month. By the end of the month, I knew which parts resonated with me and which parts to discard. That would be the most productive way to approach this book. I did not begin my journey believing in most of what you're about to learn. I don't expect you to believe without experiencing for yourself.

You don't need to believe everything that I believe in order to benefit from this book. We all know that EVERYTHING is energy, so everything discussed in this book can be thought about as energy- without all of the "new-age mumbo jumbo." The only possible new thing you may need to integrate is the understanding that we control energy with our intentions.

One more thing, I'm not a doctor, or a psychologist. The advice within this book is not meant to replace professional medical care and treatment. Energy healing, intuition and energetic hypnosis are meant to complement professional health care. Consult a physician if you feel that any part of the protocol is questionable for your health before practicing the methods you learn here.

My story

My journey into healing work is pretty typical as far as these kinds of stories go. Here's the usual recipe: Physical or emotional suffering plus looking for something more out of life equals a "dark night of the soul." This is often characterized by feeling that it is either time to drastically change your life or leave it altogether. Which eventually, at least in the best-case scenario, leads into a full awakening of some kind.

In my case I was living inside a nightmare of my own making. I was obsessed with my romantic relationship having to look a certain way. I had always been most focused on that aspect of my life. Family, friends, money, work and everything else always took a back seat to my romantic relationships. Nothing else seemed to matter except for that. Of course when that part of my life wasn't right it was all I could think about. All I wanted to do was fix it; control my partner into being the person I thought they were or wanted them to be. It was a pattern in my life- I'd fall in love, we'd be totally all over each other then my partner would suddenly just be comfortable, no longer interested in constant sex, passion and romance, while I wanted that to be the entire relationship, or even my entire life.

We all have our triggers and that was mine. One person may struggle with a physical issue, another may be obsessed with success at work, others may experience physical diseases or disorders but it all boils down to struggle being a catalyst for change. We come into our physical bodies on Earth in order to learn and experience. Prior to each lifetime, we pick something to be our focus and ask others to act out some scenarios with us. So, what feels awful is usually something we've chosen as a way to push ourselves to grow, change and evolve. Each lifetime is an encapsulated version of our larger soul lifespan. These mini lifetimes are, to our soul, the equivalent of visiting an amusement park for a day. It's just that most of us don't have this larger perspective while we're going through our struggle.

My most extreme romantic issues to date coincided with feelings of disenchantment in my job. I had worked in high-end spas all of my adult life and encountered an era where a couple of them really turned me off to the whole line of work- when I had previously loved my career. I was seeking in more ways than one. I felt that I could no longer continue living with the negative loop of obsessive thoughts constantly running through my mind plus I wanted to find something more meaningful and exciting to do for work. I was in the wretched place of choosing to either change my life or end it. The Universe heard my call for help. One day a Reiki teacher came in for a pedicure and we clicked immediately- having a great conversation and exchanging email addresses. Within a few months I signed up for a level 1 Reiki class with her and it changed everything.

Once I was attuned to Reiki, I immediately felt the energy in my hands and thought "Holy crap! There IS something more! This is what I am supposed to be doing." After that everything began to change. I don't want to give you the impression that everything just suddenly got better. I was still depressed, obsessive and interested in changing jobs. However, I began healing. I started reading everything I could on shifting my perception. Over the next few years, I learned the steps I needed to take in order to step out of my own misery. I also continued taking the other levels of Reiki and began offering sessions at the spa I was working in. I found that everything I was learning for myself was always very helpful and applicable for my clients as well.

This continued to expand until I felt that I was ready to rent a space of my own to offer energy work and go part time at the spa. It wasn't long before I was a full time healing practitioner and opened my own business. As soon as I found my purpose, the Universe unfolded before me. I had all the right clients coming my way and I was continually being pushed toward the books, classes, and lessons I needed in order to build the best possible life and healing practice I could. I've created a hypnosis recording program that has incredible results because it combines energy and intention with traditional hypnosis processes. The creation of the hypnosis program was followed by the healing modality you are about to dive into. Honestly, I created none of this alone. Each and every piece has been handed to me by the Universe and the Divine- which, incidentally, I consider to be the one in the same.

All I've done is surrender to what I'm being shown to

do. If I get chills, feel giddy or become spontaneously hypnotized I know I'm about to embark on something big. I keep following what interests and intrigues me. Sometimes I'm drawn to something on a conscious level and sometimes I consciously reject/judge something, but will feel energetically pushed toward it anyway. Then if I feel like it's something I can swing I go for it. This has led me to a life bigger than I could have imagined. Eventually my depression and obsessive issues healed themselves. And surprise, surprise- my love life is closer than ever to my dream. It is such a beautiful thing to help others by helping yourself and doing what you love. I've been shown how to develop intuitive, healing, mediumship, coaching, hypnosis, and channeling abilities. I am also incredibly excited to know that there are endless things for me to learn and explore with energy, intuition, The Shift, intention and so on. This book will cover all of those bases and more. We are truly limitless and I've only just begun to scratch the surface. Imagine the adventure you have in front of you.

This book began as a manual for my class on Essence Healing, but has become so much more. By the end of this book, you will absolutely be able to perform Essence Healing on yourself and others. However, as I began writing, I realized that it was even more important for people to be able to heal the misery in their lives on a conscious level as well. That is certainly what helped me the most. Healing energy certainly helps further the process, but our minds are the top thing that holds us back. If our mind is clinging to old ideas and beliefs, all the healing in the world won't be enough to stop our pain.

Essence: Ending Emptiness, Finding Fulfillment has evolved from a training manual for a healing modality to a training manual for life. May you find your way to happiness, one step at a time, and may this book be a beacon on your path.

Overview

Before we dive in, I'd like to give you a look at what you can expect. In Chapter One, we will explore the general things you need to know prior to exploring self-empowerment and healing practices. Concepts such as powerful intention, and grounding will lay the foundation for everything else. If you take anything from this book, this is the most effectual, life-changing way to begin accessing your whole self. This lays the groundwork for healing, intuition, empowerment and just plain feeling good.

Chapter Two focuses on personal empowerment through metaphysical concepts and practices. This opens your mind to different ways of looking at the world around you. It begins with a process you can try out for stepping into your power, plus there is a Divinely channeled message at the end of the chapter intended to activate another level of empowerment for you.

In Chapter Three I focus primarily on romantic relationships and our expectations of them. You will learn new ways to see love and its place in your life, as well as shifting your mindset on romance and sex in general.

Chapter Four covers the premise of forgiveness. Discover the difference between what you believe forgiveness to be as opposed to what it can be. This chapter will have you looking at letting go of the past in a whole new way.

Throughout Chapter Five we will delve into the concept of The Shift. If you've heard new age people mentioning this and wondered what they meant, or if you've felt something inexplicable and strange building over the last 5 years or so, this chapter will explain so much.

In Chapter Six we explore intuition. Learn how to recognize and build upon your inborn abilities, develop new ones and trust the messages you receive. This chapter explores everything from achieving the proper brainwave state to channeling Divine messages and connecting with those who have crossed over.

Chapter Seven covers everything from asking for permission before working on someone else to getting your ego out of the way so that healing can unfold for the best. Information on attunements to energy healing will also be covered in this Chapter.

Chapter Eight, includes many of the tools and techniques that can be applied within an Essence healing session in order to amplify the energy. Think of these as tools in your toolbox that your intuition will pick out for you as needed.

Chapter Nine will cover the basics on the chakra system within the body. You will learn what these energy centers represent and how they work. You'll get several tips on how to use the chakras during Essence Sessions. I'll also share my secret method for giving Chakra Readings, so you can amaze people with what you know about them without collecting any prior information.

Chapter Ten gives some background on Kundalini energy, so that you can activate it for yourself and others. This chapter also discusses the process of Kundalini Awakening and symptoms of Kundalini Syndrome.

Chapter Eleven is where it all comes together. I will lay out the exact steps you can use to perform Essence Healing. You'll learn the basic protocol for an Essence session plus integrate all of the tools you learned in Chapters Seven through Ten. We will also cover ways to use this healing for yourself and in everyday life.

Throughout Chapter Twelve you'll discover the most powerful methods of manifesting everything you desire. I've included my entire Metamorphosis Hypnosis Program for you to customize for yourself. This program combines

Essence, intention, hypnosis and The Law of Attraction. This program usually costs hundreds of dollars, but I feel it is so important, I've included the instructions and tools for you to shift your entire life here at no additional charge, on your own.

Chapter Thirteen delves into applying a level of professionalism if you were to decide to become a Healing Practitioner. Over the years, I've seen the full range of ways that intuitive and energy workers present themselves, observing what keeps clients coming back and what puts them off. Anyone who works with the public in any way may want to take a look at this chapter.

The final section includes book recommendations as well as a description and guide of the digital bonus materials that come with this book. These will help keep you moving forward on your journey both throughout the practices in this book and once you're finished it.

I sincerely hope you enjoy your odyssey through Essence, and that it creates lasting change in your life on many levels. I wish you peace, love and healing beyond your wildest dreams.

Chapter One

The Power of Intention

Throughout the course of this book I will be instructing you to envision or mentally create various things. Before you are ready or able to do this, you must understand the power of your intentions. When you intend for something to happen, it IS occurring on an energetic level. You may not witness it on the physical level yet- especially if you are not in tune with subtle energy movement. Once you begin to fully experience and interact with energy, you will bear witness to energetic shifts related to your intentions on a regular basis. Doing the practices in this book will eventually lead you to develop a heightened perception of energy. Until then, just trust, as best you can, that your intention is controlling the energy. The more you practice, the more proof you will encounter and compile.

Grounding

Grounding, the act of pulling your spirit fully into your

body, is the key element to all Essence practices. It is what makes this modality so different and so powerful. Grounding is the base for every skill you will learn in this book. It is also the number one thing that our guides want us to know how to achieve at this time.

Whether you call it your spirit, soul, energy, higher self, God-Self, prana, chi, ki or whatever- it all boils down to one thing, it is our very Essence. Over several centuries, for various reasons, we have lost touch with our true Essences and begun to live from our egos and logical minds. This creates great dis-ease within us. We become frenzied and feel a perpetual sense of lack, fear and loneliness. Learning how to bring our Essence back home to us creates peace, bliss, wisdom, and a sense of completion.

Learning how to ground has numerous benefits: it feels good, it connects you with a much deeper wisdom within you, it brings forth healing from within, and a sense of wholeness. When your Essence is within you, you feel more complete, experiencing far less addiction and need for external things to fulfill you. Grounding also acts as a protective shield against lower vibration energies that can take the form of the emotions of others, negative energy (i.e. "bad vibes"), spirits/entities/ghosts, psychic attack and so on.

The two primary components of grounding in this modality are bringing your spirit into your body and raising your vibration. Your vibration is the speed at which the molecules of your body and energy field are moving. The goal is to get them to vibrate at the highest possible frequency at any given time, as well as continually developing the ability to raise it to new heights.

There is absolutely no downside to grounding- except that you and your essence are no longer used to it, so it now takes practice and intention to achieve and maintain. However, grounding is the best possible thing you can do for yourself and others- so it's worth the effort. Eventually it becomes easier and more natural and the payoff is huge.

There is an MP3 guided meditation in the digital bonus materials that will walk you through the process of grounding, or you can try the process below.

The Grounding Process

In order to achieve the level of grounding I am referring to, I suggest the following protocol:

- Relax in a quiet place.

- Call your Essence to you and ask it to enter your physical body. Allow yourself to experience this in whatever way it comes to you. You may feel something settling in your heart and solar plexus chakra areas then expanding. It may also appear to you as a light version of you, stepping into your body.

- Feel the energy filling and surrounding you. Pay close attention to how your hands and feet feel. This will help you recognize when you're "in" later on. Ask and intend for your body and brain to be raised in vibration to resonate perfectly with your Essence.

- Observe this process with all of your senses; find out how it feels/looks/sounds to resonate at this higher vibration. Stay with this as long as you'd like.

- Allow the energy to exude from your Essence, surrounding you with higher vibration energy and bliss.

- Practice this technique whenever you think of it, are feeling off, are engaging in energy work, feel unsafe,

4

feel fearful, wish to tap into your intuition, etc.

- The more you ground, the easier it becomes. Eventually you will be able to ground while walking down the street or having a conversation. This will evolve into spontaneous connectivity over time.

Note:

Your Essence is not used to being grounded any more than you are, so it may "pop out" as quickly as it went in-especially if you don't allow your vibration to rise up to meet it and maintain that vibration. It can be quite uncomfortable for our Essence to live in our lower vibrational bodies-especially if we are commonly stressed or depressed. Think about how it feels to be around a person who is extremely high or low energy for extended periods. Now imagine trying to live inside their energy field constantly. This is how your Essence feels living in a lower vibrational body. Just keep practicing and raising your vibration as much as you can. You'll get it, and before long, your Essence will feel right at home where it belongs!

Chapter Two

Stepping into Your Power

In my workshop "You Are So Powerful!" I walk people through the process of stepping into their power. This simple exercise can go a long way toward activating confidence and abilities within you, as well as communicating to the universe that you are ready to take things up a notch.

- Stand with your feet shoulder width apart.

- Close your eyes and ground yourself.

- Envision a column of light in front of you that represents your power.

- State either silently or out loud "I now step into my power" and take a step forward.

- Allow this energy to merge with you and your energy to merge with it. Feel the energy. Breathe it in.

- Stand like this for as long as you'd like.

Note: You may also repeat this process with other intentions such as stepping into your purpose, psychic abilities, healing abilities and so on. Each activation will likely feel or look different in some way. Pay attention to any subtle cues you get as you step into various things.

Raise Your Vibration

With $E=mc^2$, Albert Einstein proved that everything is energy. We're energy, the planet we live on, everything we see, touch, smell, hear, see, taste and perceive. Even thought is energy. Quantum Physicists are proving more and more that thought, intention and energy make a difference in our physical world.

The energy of our Essence has been called many things in various cultures, Chi, Ki, Prana, Soul, Spirit, Life Force Energy, Higher Self and God Self are among a few. Any time we work with energy through intention, we create change. First, on a spiritual and energetic level, then on a physical level. Energy Healing, intuition and other energetic practices put us more in touch with the energy we are made up of.

They help us to keep our vibration high, allowing us to positively affect the world around us.

One of the best ways you can make a difference in your life and the lives of those around you is to raise your vibration. It makes you a better healer; it connects you with the divine more easily, increases wisdom, feels better and positively affects everyone and everything you interact with in any way. Below you will find a few suggestions that will help you raise your vibrational frequency- creating happiness within & around you.

- Do things you enjoy
- Surrender to what IS right now- even if it seems negative.
- Use your intention to pull your spirit/Essence/energy into your body- every time you feel "off"
- Be active/Work out/Move!
- Eat well
- Have a great sex life
- Get outside and commune with nature in whatever way appeals to you

- Let go of worrying every chance you get. If you can't fix it now, there's no value in fretting about it. You'd be better off going into meditation, listing your issue, and seeing what kind of epiphanies come to you.
- Meditate or pray
- Give or receive energy work
- Reprogram your negative self-talk and programming with hypnosis, tapping (EFT), Theta Healing, affirmations, meditation and so on…
- Beam love from your heart every chance you get.
- Scroll past the Facebook posts that bother you.
- Hug
- Play
- Dance

Personal Empowerment

When I began my journey into the metaphysical, I was anything but empowered. I was placing all of my self worth and satisfaction on other people and it felt awful. The further I've gone into the metaphysical realm, the more empowered and happy I've become. I want to share the information with

10

you that has helped me grow so immensely. Welcome to Metaphysical 101 as told by April Adams. As with everything else, take what resonates with you and leave the rest. I am no guru, I just see the value in sharing what has worked for me.

Just for the next month or so, I invite you to forget everything you've learned in our culture. Try living from a new perspective and open mind. After all, how has living with the concepts and ideals of our culture served you so far? If it is time to make a change in your life, your mind is the place to begin.

As I covered in Chapter One, our intention is everything. The power of our minds is vast and unfathomable. In the movie *What the Bleep Do We Know?* Energy, in connection with the mind, is explored in depth. I highly recommend this film, which incidentally is available for free on YouTube. There are several potent messages within the movie that I found highly enlightening.

Dr. Masaru Emoto's study on water and intention was of particular interest, as we are more than 70% water ourselves. He took different bottles of water, labeled them with positive or negative sentiments, along with intending those sentiments into that bottle and its contents. When examined under a microscope, the positively labeled bottles produced frozen samples that were beautiful and symmetrical like crystals and snowflakes. The ones with negative labels became asymmetrical, ugly and blobular. If simple intention can do this to water, what are our thoughts creating in our water-based bodies?

Another interesting point was that we train our brain synapses and body chemicals with the way we think. A tendency to think negative thoughts make the brain synapses connect to continue thinking those kinds of thoughts, which in turn, activate stress chemicals and hormones to release in our bodies. We can actually become just as addicted to negativity chemicals as we can to the pleasurable ones. This creates a dynamic in which we seek out drama and pain in order to feel something. It is possible to retrain the mind to think more positively, reconnecting the synapses in different patterns, which bring about pleasure chemicals. It takes focus on the thoughts themselves. It is important to recognize the brain as a tool and not your identity. Then you may begin catching it in the act of dwelling on negativity and redirecting it to something positive or neutral. This process can take a year or more, but it's better than a lifetime of stress and the resulting poor health that you create yourself. Don't be afraid to have a conversation with your brain- treat it like an amusing and naughty puppy or toddler that needs constant redirection. That's pretty much what it is.

Most of us have been trained to look at things from a place of fear. It's cultural, but you can break the pattern for yourself and begin living a happier healthier life. I'd like to warn you though. About halfway through this process you're going to feel super bored with life. This is due to the addiction to the rush of stress hormones your negative thoughts usually produce. As your brain and body make the shift from negative to positive, they will bridge the gap with neutrality, which feels pretty dull in comparison. Don't fight it- just go with it- recognize it's part of the process and reassure yourself that the feel good chemicals are on their way. A trick I sometimes use is picturing myself doing something that excites me, such as riding a roller coaster. I picture being at the top of that first hill and let my breath catch in my chest, allowing the giddy excitement- with just a touch of fear - overtake me. This creates a nice rush, which just may help you over the boredom hump. If roller coasters aren't your thing, get creative and think about whatever excites you. You could also try watching a comedy or one of your favorite funny videos, singing a song you love and really getting into it, going for a run, or dancing like no one's watching.

Our minds are vast and powerful. Perception plays a key role in how we interpret things. I saw a 20/20 episode about women who turned the pain of childbirth into ecstasy with their perception alone. They went into labor deciding it was a natural experience and rather than resisting the sensations and perceiving them as negative, they rode the waves and found pleasure there. Some even experienced orgasm. It is amazing to me what the mind is capable of, if we just learn how to use it to our advantage.

A tool that I share with my clients is picturing a control panel in your mind of all of your body's hormones and chemicals. Create a dial for each of the following: Dopamine for confidence, rewards and bliss, Oxytocin for trust and openness, Endorphins for euphoria, pain relief and stress relief, Serotonin for feeling calm and valued or sleepy, Adrenaline for excitement or nervousness, Cortisol for stress or that knot in your stomach and so on. You can even simplify, if you're not familiar with the body's chemicals, by labeling each dial with an emotion instead. Now that you've got this mental control panel, turn the ones you want way up and the ones you don't want way down. I love the soothing effect of turning my cortisol off. It's pretty amazing what our brains are capable of.

A great way to make life feel less negative is to ask yourself: "What would happen if I looked at everything as a neutral experience? Nothing good or bad, just another experience on the plate of life?" If you weren't busy judging each experience, wouldn't things feel better overall? As human beings, we are constantly in a state of judgment. This is partially the fault of biology, partially the fault of our ego and partially the fault of programming we receive from others as we've grown up. Biologically, we're designed to look out for attack and things that could harm us. The ego serves a similar purpose, creating a dynamic of self-preservation. As we grew up in our society, we were taught to judge everything from foods to clothing, to our bodies, to political parties. Who taught you to judge? How much of your life do you spend resisting what is? What if you let go of these judgments and any stubbornness?

I know someone who gets upset at the mere mention of marijuana, even if someone is just joking about it or making an off-hand comment. I'm not referring to a situation in which it's being offered to him, or used in his presence. It really ticks him off and sends him spiraling into a dark mood and a negative loop of thoughts activating stress chemicals in his body. Is it worth this trauma, pain and health risk to get so caught up in such judgments?

I used to be triggered in the same way if someone played music they knew I didn't like. I would become sullen, angry and hurt. In the end, this did nothing but cause me pain. I could have taken a step back and thought about the other persons enjoyment of the music, or recognized the possibility that they weren't even thinking about the music or the fact that I didn't enjoy it. I could have neutrally listened to the song or album to see if a different opinion might form, or even used the time to pay attention to my surroundings, be in the moment, or meditate. Unfortunately, I had no idea this was even possible. There was no end to what used to trigger me into anger, sadness or resentment.

How has it served you to let yourself be triggered? We all have certain things we've decided aren't okay with us. Our genetic programming has us reacting to things like music and conversation topics as though they are as much of a threat as a wild animal stalking us. Evolution has not caught up with our lives yet. The way out is to take a different perspective on it. Look at the other person's point of view, ask yourself if it's really worth getting worked up over, switch your focus to some other topic. Do whatever it takes to let go of the stubborn tendency to judge or get wrapped up in every little thing. Start with the small stuff and work your way up. The more you do this, the easier and more natural it will become. In Wayne Dyer's book *Your Erroneous Zones*, he covers all manner of ways we perceive things in mindsets that harm us and hold us back. I highly recommend it. If you find there are certain things you can't release as triggers, check out the Metamorphosis information in Chapter Twelve of *Essence* for an intensive method for releasing old programming.

Another thing that keeps us in a repetitive pattern of judgment is whether something is intense enough for us or not. For some, things may even be too intense, bringing up resistance. Either way, you are creating your own hell by resisting what is. If you are always looking for intensity in your foods, activities and romantic life, chances are you have an addiction to intensity. It takes time, effort and focus to end this addictive cycle, but it is so worth it. The first step to this is surrendering to what is. Completely allowing everything just as it is in this moment without judging it as good or bad. The same goes for those who fear intensity- especially in their emotions. If you begin to feel a negative emotion and try to push it down and suppress it, it will only grow bigger. You must allow your feelings and emotions to be felt in your body. Don't dwell on the thoughts- those should be redirected, but the emotions need to be completely allowed, experienced and felt. The more you can allow your emotions, the faster they will heal and move on. Panic attacks are usually due to a resistance of the negative emotion trying to express itself. After a while, the pressure builds up so much it has to come out somewhere and then it becomes a full-blown attack instead of an emotion.

We are so entrained to avoid our emotions that we become fearful of them. As though it would be the end of the world to sit with them. However, when you actually begin to embrace and experience all of your emotions as physical sensations in your body, you begin to realize how similar they all are. The fear is removed once you face your feelings head on, because you realize that it's not nearly as bad as you expected. Next time you're feeling angry, sad or afraid, tune into your body and feel where that emotion is sitting. Feel that physical sensation. Be with it. Open to it. Merge with it. Notice what happens. Try this a few times and you will likely stop pushing away your "negative" emotions. You may even find that you're more easily able to access your "positive" emotions.

Our emotions are meant to be a compass for us. We are born with an internal guidance system, but are trained throughout our lives to suppress it. We were taught to ignore our feelings in order to fit into our culture and make others comfortable. We've abandoned our internal compass in favor of manners and logic. Try viewing your positive feelings as guiding you toward what is meant for you and what resonates with your true self, while negative feelings are there to guide you away from things that don't resonate. This goes for reactions to people, places, thoughts and situations. It is important to pay attention to your feelings and appreciate them rather than ignoring and suppressing them.

For those addicted to intensity, consider this: What if you looked at the small moments as though they were big ones? Would your life really be wasted if your life weren't constantly intense? This was a big one for me. I wanted my romantic relationships to overwhelm me in every positive way, but often let them overwhelm me in every negative way. I had to shift my entire perspective on life and relationships in order to heal the addictive tendency within me. There were two books that were of great help in this process: *One Soul, One Love, One Heart* by John Welshons and *The 5 Love Languages* by Gary Chapman.

Many of us spend our lives focused on success in one

realm or another. We convince ourselves that we can't be happy until we have whatever it is we've set our hearts on. For some it is success at work, for others a passionate relationship, for others a certain amount of money and so on. What's your "I'll be happy when..." goal? What if, instead, you set your sights on being happy, or at least at peace, no matter what? Longing for something and resisting what is, only creates misery. When you are miserable, you are not resonating with your Essence or your desires, you are resonating with not having them- because that's what you're focused on. Focusing on what you don't want or don't have will only bring you more of the same.

What I'd like to propose as an alternative is finding ways to fulfill yourself and make yourself happy no matter what. Do things you enjoy now. Follow your gut to exploring new things. Appreciate what you do have. In our culture, there is an odd belief that it is selfish to focus on your own happiness. When in actuality, making yourself happy and fulfilled is the best thing you can do for everyone. The happier and more fulfilled you are, the higher your vibration is and the more you have to share with others. The higher your vibration, the better people feel around you. The better they feel, the higher their vibrations go, creating a ripple effect around the community and then the planet. As an extra added bonus, the more you surrender to the way things are and take care of raising your own vibration, the more you get of what you wanted in the first place. The old saying "If you love someone, set them free," is very apropos here, as you often have to let go of your obsession with what you desire in order to get it.

> *Tell everyone you know: "My happiness depends on me, so you're off the hook." And then demonstrate it. Be happy, no matter what they're doing. Practice feeling good, no matter what. And before you know it, you will not give anyone else responsibility for the way you feel -- and then, you'll love them all. Because the only reason you don't love them, is because you're using them as your excuse to not feel good.*
>
> -Abraham Hicks

In *The Power of Now*, Eckhart Tolle discusses the ego at length. In the metaphysical world, the ego is the part of us that is always judging everything. Tolle asserts that by being in the moment and surrendering to what is happening right now, we begin to move past the pain and limitation that the ego creates. When we first begin this journey, it can often feel as though we are losing our sense of self because we are so used to our ego running the show and forming opinions on everything.

In the Buddhist faith, there is a different concept of sin, Heaven and Hell than what we typically think of. Sin is actually the Latin word for mistake. If you look closely at the primary sins we focus on in our culture, we see that they are generally perpetrated by the ego. When we commit a "sin" we are creating Hell on earth for ourselves. What we need to know is that we can create Heaven on earth for ourselves as well- just by being mindful, grateful and as in the moment as possible. The more we focus on negativity, the deeper into a Hell of our own making we go. Our reward or punishment is not put off until our death, it's right here in the present moment. You have to choose, in every moment, where you'd rather be.

One more thing about judgment and energy: We each carry our beliefs about ourselves within our energy fields. To others, this acts like a big neon sign above us that their subconscious mind reads, sending an instant message of judgment to their brain. For example: Let's say a large woman walks by and you're suddenly thinking "Look at that fatty." You then wonder why you thought that, as you generally have no issue with overweight people and their bodies. A few minutes later an even larger woman walks by and you think "I like her dress." So why the discrepancy? The first woman likely tells herself she is fat, ugly, disgusting and so on, while the second woman generally feels confident and embraces her body and looks. They have these feelings in their energy fields and you've picked them up like a radio signal and allowed your brain to translate their energy into your perception of them.

Sometimes it's not all them though. If you really get worked up over it, it's more about you. Let's say you see either woman and start to feel sadness, anger or disgust toward her that you get wrapped up in. This reaction likely means that you have issues with your own weight- either that you are upset with yourself for letting yourself go, or alternately, you may feel jealous that she lets herself be that way, while you work so hard to stay fit, denying yourself the things she allows herself. Perhaps you could benefit from an occasional treat, rather than being so strict with yourself. Next time you have a knee-jerk reaction to someone, take a deeper look into it. If it's fleeting and weird, it's about them, if it persists and triggers you, it's telling you something about yourself.

We often attract people who are similar to us in some way to provide mirrors into ourselves. If you really like something about someone, it is likely they are showing you an aspect of yourself that you like. Conversely, if someone drives you crazy, they are showing you one of two things. Either you do the thing that drives you crazy about them, but secretly hate that you do it. Or, they are showing you a part of yourself you won't allow. For example: Let's say you're a Type A personality who has to do everything right and is constantly trying to make everyone happy. You have a coworker who is very laid back, failing to hold themselves to the same standard as you. This person has been brought into your experience as a signal that you're denying something within yourself. You judge them as lazy or incompetent, when actually you could greatly benefit from adopting a portion of their behavior or attitude. After all, how healthy is it to have to be perfect at everything? That level of effort isn't beneficial for anyone. You don't need to suddenly become them, but allowing a bit more relaxation into your life and attitude could go a long way toward improving your life.

The way this showed up in my life was with pushy, demanding women coming to me for spa services. They'd plunk down in front of me and very precisely tell me what they wanted me to do for them. At that time in my life, I had no idea at all how to stand up for myself or ask for what I desired. I knew what I wanted or deserved, but would rarely do anything about it externally. I remember thinking "How dare she?" many times. How dare she what? Ask for what she wants from a service provider? Ha! These women drove me batty and they kept showing up until I got the point. I slowly began to ask for what I wanted and saying no when I needed to in daily situations. I was more tactful about it, but it still got the job done. The more I stood up for myself in all aspects of my life, the less pushy they became toward me. Amazing.

A Divine Message

Perhaps the most empowering and exciting thing of all is that we are loved beyond measure by All That Is. Our Guides, Souls Families, Source and so on have so much love, respect and reverence for us. They are blown away by our bravery to incarnate into this physical plane in physical bodies. The energy I feel emanating from them in sessions and in channels is huge and beautiful. Allow me to channel a message for you here. Surrender into feeling the words and the energy.

"We love and adore you. You are an incredible being to be where you are at such a time as this. All that you are and all that you will ever be is magical, beautiful and powerful. We wish to bless you with our presence and assistance in every moment, if you will allow it and call upon us- not only in times of need but every chance you get. We are here for you. You are astoundingly powerful beyond anything you can currently perceive. We are in awe of your human journey and fortitude. You are glorious and miraculous, as are all beings derived from Spirit, The Universe, The Divine. What you choose to do from this moment forward is a matter of your own free will, yet we encourage you to follow your bliss. Let go of trying to please those around you or getting the approval of others. Loving yourself and your life will attract those who love you for who and what you are. You will inspire them to shine their light and to pass that inspiration on to others, creating a chain reaction beyond your realm of understanding. Let go of suffering and victimhood. The time for this has passed. It is a time to explore, grow and celebrate. We send you love, peace and warm regards beyond all language. Be blessed. Namaste."

You are the architect of your own life. How will you design it?

Chapter Three

Relationships

It is most certainly not up to me how you live your life or function in your relationships. However, I struggled so much in this area of my life for so long, that finding my way out of my old mindset was the most empowering and rewarding thing I've ever done. I want to share the premises that helped me find my way out of the pit.

Look at the way love is presented to us. Love songs, breakup songs, romance novels, movies, TV, "reality" shows all give us our culture's idea of how love should look. I was weaned on the stuff. I've been obsessed with love and all of its trimmings from an inappropriately young age- in truth it was all that mattered to me from preschool until just a few years ago. If my love life didn't look exactly the way I expected it to, it was the end of the world. This came to a head for me when I met the most special person and fell instantaneously in love. We were crazy for each other and discovered tantric sex without having the first clue about

Tantra. We saw every lifetime in each other's eyes. I knew I had to make this a permanent part of my life. Of course this required both of us to make drastic changes in our already established lives, so the very transition meant to bring us closer changed the dynamic of what made us so special. Hence the beginning of the dark night of my soul. It took me three years of misery and resistance before I realized the problem was in how I was looking at things, not in the relationship itself. Since I began applying the principles I'll be sharing here, every aspect of my life has drastically improved. And yes, my relationship has too. I hope it helps you just as much.

Everything we encounter in our culture regarding love ruins us for the actual experience. Our expectation for another person to complete us and provide our happiness robs us of the ability to truly love. What most of us are looking for is infatuation, passion, romance and the like. These are not love. They can be aspects of the love experience, but they don't define it. I am not here to define love for you either. Your heart and soul already know love. You must get in touch with those parts of yourself in order to discover the meaning of true love within yourself.

It took me a while to get this, but nobody else was put here to make me happy. I had to do that for myself. My whole life I been taught that someone else would make me happy but it never happened for more than a year at a time. Once the newness wore off, I was lost. I was addicted to so many aspects of new love (infatuation), that it was like going through withdrawal from drugs every time that phase ended.

I also needed infatuation to feed my ego. I was taught that it wasn't okay to compliment myself- that was vanity/pride/bragging. So I had to have someone obsessed with, complimenting and desiring me in order to feel valid, valued and loved. Without someone chasing me around all day, how was I to know I was sexy, attractive or worthy?

When I was struggling in my relationship, I logically knew that I was loved, even though I couldn't feel it- due to my own perception and programming. In fact, my relationship was the healthiest one I had ever experienced or witnessed. That's how I knew it was me and not the relationship that needed to change.

Once I'd taken a step back and examined my romantic

patterns, I finally realized that the repetitive issues in my life were nobody's fault but my own. This realization led me to my discovery of Reiki and inspired my entire metaphysical journey. I realized that I needed to find something just for me, rather than focusing all of my attention on my love life. I'd always been interested in metaphysical ideas, but hadn't had much exposure to them. When a Reiki class came up, I took it and never turned back. I also began reading everything I could get my hands on.

Eckhart Tolle's *The Power of Now* and John Welshons *One Soul, One Love, One Heart* were among the first of my life-preservers toward a new way of thinking, seeing and feeling. Whenever I was struggling, I would distract myself by reading something to shift my perception and remove me from my negative thought patterns. Books saved my life and my marriage. It was a long journey out of the deep depression I had put myself into, but as long as I had something I could read every time I noticed myself dwelling on my favorite topic with negative obsessive thinking, I found my way out again and again. Each time I got out of the emotional pit it lasted longer and each time I fell in was shorter and less intense. It wasn't a quick journey- five years in all, I'd say, but it was so worth it, as I am immensely happy with my life now.

Take a look at your relationships. Have you put expectations on your partner(s) to behave a certain way toward you? Have you tried to control their behavior? Have you been loved and respected, but just not felt the passion you'd like to have? Have you been giving them what you'd like to receive from them, hoping they'll get the hint and start giving it back to you, but feeling resentful that they don't? We've all been there. It's time to set yourself and your partner free. You have to realize that it is your expectations making you miserable, not the behavior of others. Stop putting ANY expectations of any kind on them and go make yourself happy. All you really want is to feel good; you've just been taught that love is the only way to get there. What you weren't taught is that self-love is the way there - not "other love."

Now is the time for you to please you. Think about how you'd feel if you got what you wanted from your partner. What emotions would you feel? That's what you're actually looking for- those feelings. The circumstances that bring them about actually don't matter. So start looking for ways you can give yourself those kinds of feelings. Explore interests you've had, but not fully delved into yet. Start doing things you used to love, but got too busy or distracted to do. Try new things. Discover your passion. Look for classes, books, clubs and so on that draw your interest. Once you begin exploring, the journey begins to unfold itself. The deeper you get into feeding your soul, the less pressure you put on your love life. The less pressure you put on your partner, the more relaxed and open they become.

Another dynamic unfolding on an energetic level is that you are now treating yourself the way you'd like to be treated. You're no longer wearing an energetic sign that says "needy" on it, so everyone begins to interact with you differently. You may find the negative people in your life pulling back and more positive interactions finding their way to you. Best of all, your partner begins to see you differently and interacts with you on a level closer to your desires. This change occurs over time and becomes better and better the more you fulfill yourself and the less pressure you apply.

An extra added bonus is that you have much more to share with others when your own cup is full. When you look to others to fill you up, there is no way of knowing when you'll receive your next refill. When it's you, you can pour some more in whenever you want to. This creates a feeling of fullness and gratitude within you, which in turn, raises your vibration. It can also inspire more generosity on your part. If you always feel like you're lacking, you don't feel you have enough to give others, but this disappears when your love cup is full. The misery of not having what you want is often the very catalyst that inspires you to live your soul's purpose here.

There's a great book called *The 5 Love Languages* by Gary Chapman that revolutionized the way I see relationships. The night I finished reading this book I closed my eyes to go to sleep and had every moment in my relationship in which I felt hurt, rejected or destroyed pop up in front of my eyes and turn itself around into this new perspective. This process occurred for about 45 minutes. I laid there in awe, realizing that my perception had caused way more pain than was necessary or intended. It went a long way toward healing my romantic relationship, as well as helping me to understand everyone I interact with on a deeper level.

The premise is that we each have a primary love language that we most easily communicate our love with. The languages are words, touch, acts of service, quality time, and gift giving. I'd like to add a 6th for those who were sexualized early - sex. In the beginning we often speak all of these to each other because of the hormones and excitement of it all. Once we get past the infatuation period, we tend to revert back to our one original language. This often leaves one or both partners feeling unloved unless they speak the same innate language. Imagine speaking Spanish while your partner speaks Japanese. It's the same as if you prefer touch and your partner uses words. I highly recommend this book if you struggle in romantic relationships. It can make a difference even if your partner doesn't read it.

When you communicate with anyone regarding your needs, it is important that you leave out any blame. Put it all on you, your feelings and desires. Let go of the tendency to ask why they do or don't do something. State your needs and desires in such a way that they understand you're sharing yourself with them, rather than blaming them for not reading your mind. This is a great way to express yourself without rocking the boat. Your partner may fear intimate talks because they are used to being attacked or blamed. What if you could just state the facts rather than pointing fingers? What would that change?

If nothing else, energetically, you must resonate with something in order to attract it. If you resonate with need, you advertise and attract need. If you resonate with happiness, peace and fulfillment you advertise and attract those qualities and experiences. This is the essence of Essence Healing. Resonate with your higher self, which resonates with your desires manifested, then you attract what you most desire. Focus on what you want rather than what you don't.

You must also recognize that you are dealing with a whole other person, with their own purpose, goals, desires and programming. Expecting them to devote their life to pleasing you is the ultimate in narcissism. Not that you need to beat yourself up over it. It's the way we've been programmed to be. But we have to begin realizing that relationships are not there to complete us. True soulmate connections will test us and push us in ways we never expected. Relationships are our biggest, most important classrooms.

Sex

There is much confusion with this topic because most of us understand on some core level that sexual connectivity is important and sacred. This is the absolute truth. However, our culture has skewed the meaning of sex to such an extent that it has become depraved, distorted and misused. We see it as power, obligation, a means to an end, instant gratification, sin, and so on. It is meant to be balancing, creating (both of life and of energy), blissful, connective and sacred.

This is a time of learning to balance the power and energy of masculine and feminine energy, to get them to work together to create a higher dimension of being. A question frequently asked is "What about same sex couples?" And the answer is that through intention we can create the balance of masculine and feminine with our energy. It takes more focus and concentration on behalf of same sex couplings, but the energetic spark is still more than possible.

I suggest working first on doing the work to release the programming of our culture and your egoic expectations of sex. Then you are ready to meet soul to soul with another being. Invite the Divine into your bedroom. Ground. Look into your lover by gazing gently at one another. Intend that your energies merge as your bodies do, balancing masculine and feminine energies for the highest good. Envision the masculine phallus entering the sacred feminine chalice, whether this is physically possible or not. Energetically all things are possible. Allow energy to flow through you both. Observe your partner, your feelings, the energy. Lose yourself in the sacred exchange. This is the way sex was intended to be. All else is child's play. (The last few paragraphs were 95% channeled, so that was them saying child's play - not me.)

Abuse

While I highly recommend working through your relationship issues, rather than running from person to person looking for fulfillment, I would NEVER suggest staying in a relationship in which you are chronically disrespected or abused in any way. This is far different than expecting someone to complete you. Commanding respect and safety are the first priority and a huge part of your own empowerment. If you don't feel safe or nurtured, you should find a way to leave immediately.

Chapter Four

Forgiveness

In our culture, we tend to think of forgiveness as taking the high road or letting someone off the hook. In the metaphysical belief system it's about letting go of something so that you can heal. Have you heard the saying "Anger is like pouring poison for someone else and drinking it yourself"? When we hold a grudge against someone, it isn't doing anything to them, but all kinds of awful things to us. If we dwell on their behavior and the pain they caused us, we continue doing to ourselves what they did to us. Our brain has no way of differentiating between an actual situation happening in front of us and a situation we're thinking about. Our body will react the same way to a thought as it would to a live situation.

If you keep replaying the crime and playing the victim, you are harming yourself in myriad ways. First you are programing your brain to think negatively, which produces stress chemicals and creates a pattern of future negative thoughts and chemicals, eventually bringing about health issues. It creates a situation in your brain in which the crime is being perpetuated against you again and again- triggering your fight or flight response and riling you up all over again each time you think about it. It also keeps you believing you are powerless, which you are not.

Aside from the obvious, there are some deeper things to consider about forgiveness. Each person is operating from the standpoint of their own experience and perception. What was their childhood like? What has their experience taught them? Take into consideration that they were raised by different people, have a different genetic make-up, have a chemical imbalance, or have had experiences that taught them to behave in such a way. We all do the best with what we are given. If you made a mistake or hurt someone, wouldn't you want the same consideration?

Going even deeper, it is believed that we set up the major players in our life before we are born into a body. We ask members of our soul family to play certain parts in our lives so that we can learn or experience something. It is quite likely that if someone is really pushing your buttons, you asked them to, for your highest good. It may look awful and not make sense as it's unfolding, but in the end it helps you grow. You've likely played catalyst for others as well. This all plays out on a subconscious level so that we can be as enmeshed in the journey of our physical life as possible.

Another level of this is connected to the idea I discussed earlier about people mirroring us. Sometimes we attract certain behaviors from others as a mirror to our current vibration and us. Whatever energy we put out comes back to us amplified to give us a glaring example of what kind of energy we're putting out into the world. This isn't always the reason someone may mistreat you, but it's worth pondering.

In the end, forgiveness is letting go of something that someone did to you because you have better things to do than let those past moments hold you back in any way. The same goes for forgiving yourself for anything you've done to yourself and others. Now you know better and you can do better. Everyone will be much better served by you moving on and living happily, placing more positive energy and love into the world. Oh and they do say happiness and success are the best revenge.

Speaking of happiness we've been taught that we should be charitable and do for others, which is fine- unless we are so overwhelmed we have nothing left to give. We are entrained to make others comfortable by stifling our own emotions and impulses. The very emotions and impulses that were meant to help us live our Soul's purpose and the happiest lives possible. When we shut this down, we shut down our soul. We learn to live from ego and logic only, which leaves us cold, frustrated, empty and resentful.

I'd like to point out that there are many ways to be helpful to others. Giving to charities, going out of your way to do something nice for someone, donating your time to a cause, entertaining people, healing people and so on. Whatever it is you choose to do, make sure it's not out of a sense of obligation or pressure. Such actions deplete you and contribute negative energy to whatever you're doing. There is a reason you feel drawn to some things and not others. Do not allow others to make you feel guilty about the way you choose to contribute to the world. We all have gifts and things we're drawn to. These are signals pointing us to our purpose. The more we live our purpose and the happier we are, the more we have to give. The better we feel, the higher our vibration is. Our energetic vibration flows outward to those around us and to the planet itself. It's important to keep your focus on what sparks you and allow others to do the same. It's nobody's business but yours how you choose to contribute to society. Even if your only contribution is holding a high vibrational frequency by being happy, you are contributing in a HUGE way.

Chapter Five

The Shift

The premise of the Shift is that the vibrational frequency of the Earth is being raised right now. It is part of the evolution of the planet and is also connected to the recent planetary alignments within our solar system. However, there is a metaphysical aspect to this as well. Allow me to fill in some back-story here.

There has been a vast array of channeled information coming in over the last 30-40 years leading us into the Shift, which explains a lot about our purpose and the nature of our existence on Earth. From what I've pieced together from various channels, including some of my own, this is the version that resonates most deeply with me: We are, at our core, energetic/spirit beings who, in our natural state, are one with each other and Source (God.) We collectively created physical realms, of which the Earth is one of the most intensely challenging. These various planes were created for us to be able to play out and experience separation, physical limitation, physical pleasure and myriad other things we don't experience while we're just grooving together in the ethers.

It is believed that, in the beginning, we were incarnating as physical beings, but at some point in our lives, many of us would "wake up" in the physical "dream" and recognize that it was just a play we were acting out, which caused us to lose the realness of our experience, allowing us to detach from our physical experience of choice and miss out on the point of coming here in the first place. The solution we collectively chose was the Dark Ages, in which the politicians and priests in power rewrote sacred texts so that the few could control the many. At this point in history, many Christian texts were altered from their true and original forms into controlling, fear based rhetoric. They then proceeded to hunt down, punish, torture and kill anyone who displayed any sense of personal empowerment through spirituality, healing or intuitive gifts. The deeper, more divine purpose was keeping us asleep, but it's time now to wake up. When the fear that resulted from the Dark Ages began to dissipate, we then transitioned into the Age of

Reason/Enlightenment - which basically dismissed anything that couldn't be seen under a microscope. The Shift marks the end of this repression. At some point, we looked around and realized that we'd made a mess of things, letting ego and separation take over. This is a time of collectively moving out of the dark and into the dynamic of "as above, so below."

Did you get caught up in the idea of the world ending in 2012? The Mayan calendar ended in December of 2012, so many believed this was a prediction of the end of the world. However, it is actually believed to be a prediction of the end of one era and the beginning of a new one. 12.12.12 or 12.21.12 were significant dates of vibrational shifts on Earth related to planetary alignments and the awakening of many people. This is meant to be a time of change, an opportunity to create Heaven on Earth.

In *The Three Waves of Volunteers And The New Earth*, Dolores Cannon discusses three separate groups of souls who took physical form in shifts over the last 50 years or so. The first group made way for later volunteers by beginning to reintroduce the "truth" through new ideas. John Lennon is a good example of someone from the first wave of volunteers. The next batch of volunteers would now fall between the ages of 25 and 50. The purpose of these people is simply to raise the vibration of people and the planet, by maintaining their own high vibration and allowing it to resonate outward. This group doesn't need to do anything but vibrate well - but the best possible way to do this is by doing what they love and following their souls guidance to what feels good for them. The final group is comprised mainly of the special and gifted children coming in over the last 25 years. They are meant to use their individual gifts to affect actual change on the planet as the systems that are currently in place, but no longer functioning for the highest good, begin to deteriorate. Many of them will be psychic or display inborn healing abilities, but those aren't the only markers. Several of them are diagnosed as autistic, ADHD and other special needs. These are meant to be gifts. Unfortunately, our culture has tried to mold them into well-rounded beings who fit in, rather than allowing them to cultivate their own specialties and interests. When that changes, they will flourish and help create a new world for the rest of us.

Part of this transition is marked by many people returning to their gifts and abilities. So many of my clients came to me after beginning to spontaneously develop their intuitive abilities saying that they had started hearing, seeing and feeling unusual things. They worried that they were crazy or sick. They had visited doctors who told them nothing was wrong with them. Imagine their relief when I informed them that they were just awakening. Watch for mystery symptoms you may be experiencing as you open energetically. The higher vibration of the planet is opening us all more than we've been in centuries, and it's happening faster and faster as it gains momentum. What took a year to manifest before, now takes a month. Buckle your seat belt now, because it's likely that the information and energy in this book will be a catalyst to your acceleration.

For some, the Shift is uncomfortable. When the planet you live on is vibrating at a different frequency than it has been, or is vibrating on a different frequency than you are, it doesn't feel good. The even more difficult part of this is that we don't recognize this on a conscious level, but rather subconsciously. This creates an underlying feeling of fear, confusion and unease. The best thing you can do to ease your transition into the shift is raising your vibration. This will allow you to resonate more closely with the planet as well as your spirit. This is why being in touch with your Essence and its frequency is so important and pleasant. Another thing you can do to make things more comfortable is to surrender to whatever is occurring. As we discussed in the section on ego and judgment, trying to control things to go as we expect them to just creates frustration and drama- which lowers our vibration. The more you can go with the flow, the better you will feel and the more help you'll be to others going through the shift.

We also need to be aware that everyone on Earth is connected and if there is a lot of fear happening across the globe, we are going to feel it. Even if we're able to maintain a level of zen, we still pick up on the collective energy. Grounding is a big help and so is intentionally pulling in the tendrils of your energy. My favorite method is to picture your energy field as an octopus that has its tentacles all over everyone. Tell it to pull in those tentacles and mind its own business. You don't help anyone by taking on their fear. If you want to help, stop allowing yourself to swim in their misery and keep yourself at a higher resonance. If you want to be even more helpful, you can send Essence Healing to everyone, by picturing it expanding out around you further and further until the whole planet and everyone on it is filled and surrounded by this high vibration energy. There will be more on that in later chapters.

As the Shift continues, we will develop more and more skills and abilities and become even more connected. Make sure to keep your intention on that high vibration and share the love. There will be people who do not wish to change as the planet does. It is not your job to convince them to do anything, or to fix them in any way. We each have free will as to how we choose to live our lives. If you like having the freedom to choose your path, you must allow others to do the same. Not everyone will even take the same path to change - so when people have different routes or beliefs, let them go along their path. We will all get where we are meant to be. An ability to surrender and a high vibration just make the journey more comfortable.

Many channels have been focusing on wiping the slate

clean. Basically, it is understood that we chose to come to Earth only to experience. That is our top priority and directive. Under this idea, nothing we have ever done or could ever do is wrong or bad. Being in a physical body on a physical planet allows us to experience things we cannot experience in energy/spirit form. It is a short visit in the grand scheme of our total existence. Some experiences and actions are more pleasant than others, but they are all equal in the eyes of Spirit. It is all part of the rich tapestry of being alive. Finding ways to playfully explore our physical existence and let go of our intense societal programming is a huge way to move toward joy.

When I began my journey into metaphysics and energy I was frustrated that I hadn't discovered it sooner. I actually get this from older clients who are awakening right now too. There is a feeling of "If I had only known sooner..." However, the world wasn't ready for this yet. If I had discovered this sooner, I would have quickly become frustrated with trying to develop a practice in a culture that wasn't open to such things. The Shift is creating an energy of openness and awakening in many people right at this very moment. This is the exact time you were meant to receive this information and awakening. It is all unfolding perfectly.

Why "Bad" Things Happen

There are many different takes on the shift and where things are headed. I believe that we are heading for great change. Our financial, medical, educational, religious, and governing systems are in for some major upheaval. Keep in mind that this may look scary and create great fear in people. Change is scary for most people. All you can do is continue acknowledging that the chaos you are seeing will shift things into a better way in the future. Keep grounding and raising that vibration. Everything will turn out for the best.

Another example of negatively perceived events being divinely guided are all of the frightening events we've had such as 9/11, school shootings, marathon bombings and so on. All of these were actually orchestrated by the Divine in order to remind us of our oneness and to bring us together as a collective/community. What looks like pure evil can actually divinely inspire the greatest moments of love and connection between human beings. As humans, it is hard for us to step back and see the beauty behind these tragedies. But it's there. If you can acknowledge your divinity and look at the bigger picture you'll see it.

Remember how we pulled together after 9/11? Remember the hockey game after the Boston Marathon bombing where the famous opera singer dedicated the national anthem to the bombing victims and proceeded to step back as the entire audience began singing as one, with all their hearts? Remember the interviews of the families of the Sandy Hook victims, where they talked about the children who died? Those were some of the most awake and enlightened children on the planet. They came, unconsciously knowing their purpose, and they loved until they left. Remember how the community and the country pulled together to send light to that community for their loss? There is beauty behind everything. I understand that we have difficulty with this concept because we are so connected to our physical existence. But to our souls, this lifetime is the equivalent of a trip to an amusement park. You have to decide whether you're going to make it a fun visit or a frustrating one. You are the only one who can do that for you, just remember that whatever you decide affects the world around you. No pressure or anything…

In March of 2014 I did a speaking engagement in New York where I channeled the information that all of the things we label as bad for us are actually preparing us for the future. Microwave rays, Wi-Fi rays, GMOs, pesticides, processed foods and so on are helping us become like cockroaches, more and more able to survive anything as we evolve. All of these agents are helping us get stronger and more able to thrive against all odds. The intuitive channeler Lisa Gawlas mentions something similar in her blog as well. When you see multiple channelers coming up with the same information, you know it's important.

For more channeled information regarding humanity and The Shift, check out Lee Harris, Story Waters, Lisa Gawlas, The Seth Books by Jane Roberts, *The Disappearance of the Universe* by Gary Renard and *The Three Waves of Volunteers and the New Earth* by Dolores Cannon. You will find that each of these channelers brings through slightly different information, but the overlying theme is the same.

That is because the information gets translated for each of the channelers in ways that mesh with their own programs and beliefs so they can process them. As far the details, you have to trust your intuition to show you what resonates and what doesn't.

Chapter Six

Intuition

In order to live the most fulfilling life and give the best healing sessions, it is imperative that you develop your intuition. Imagine being able to receive guidance on what step you should take next in life without having to pay someone else. Picture having access to your inner truth meter in various situations. Envision having flashes of simply knowing or understanding something without even trying. You don't need to have a goal of giving readings in order to develop your intuition. It can enhance every aspect of your life. I believe that both intuition and healing abilities are our birthright. We simply didn't have anyone to teach us how to access these abilities before.

It has taken me years to get to the level of intuitive abilities I currently have, and I have miles to go in comparison to some others. These abilities and your trust in them will not come overnight. Take your time and practice as much as you can.

The first step toward accessing your inner knowing or contacting the Divine is entering the Theta brainwave state. Theta is the "gear" our minds are in when we are dreaming, hypnotized, daydreaming, entranced, deeply meditating or half asleep. This brainwave state is slower than the typical Beta or Alpha states we are most often in, and is not quite as deep as Delta- where we are so deeply asleep we're not even dreaming. Theta is the most open and connected state we can be in while still having conscious thought. Theta grants us better access to our right (creative mind) brain and our subconscious. Occasionally we can even access the unconscious and collective unconscious from this state. To me, the collective unconscious, the Akashic Records, and the divine realm are all the same thing being defined from different perspectives.

I went through a phase early in my metaphysical career where I was begging the Universe for clairvoyance and other psychic abilities. At that time, the only thing my guides would say to me in channel was "meditate, meditate, meditate." I found meditation impossible however, as I have a very busy brain. So they made things interesting for me. I

60

was signed up to do my first 5k on a specific weekend and later found out that there was a Presence Meditation Techniques class being taught by a local healing practitioner. I wanted to take the class, but had already committed to the 5k. While training, I injured my ankle. The more I tried to work with it, the worse it got. Finally I gave up on the 5k and signed up for the class. The next day my ankle was fine. Then, 3 days before the class, I woke up from a dream and what had been a road in my dream became a path of books in my half awake state. I asked my guides if I was supposed to be reading something and got a yes. I went on Amazon & started perusing the metaphysical section, asking my guides to give me a sign when I found the book. I got a text in the middle of my search & was suddenly being hypnotized. My head drooped forward, my body was relaxed. I pushed past my slowed consciousness to quickly reply to the text so I could see what was on the computer screen. I forced my head up and at the top of the screen was the book *Theta Healing* by Vienna Stibal. I clicked "take a look inside" and began to read her journey into healing work. As I read, my mind was dismissing it as just another

61

healer's story, but I was, once again, slipping into a trance. I asked if this was the book they wanted me to read and got a yes. I was immediately engrossed, and a few days later at the weekend Presence training, I realized we were being brought into Theta with the techniques we were being taught. The teacher didn't know what Theta was; she was just teaching meditation.

I pretty much spent that year having Theta thrust upon me until I got good enough to drop into the zone at will. It has served my clientele and me well. Entering Theta is the first step to nearly everything I teach or offer. It can most certainly be helpful in Essence sessions as well.

The first thing you need to know about entering Theta is that everyone can do it. If you can dream or drift off to sleep, you are capable of entering this state. Do you remember daydreaming or going into a daze as a child? That was Theta. There are different levels of depth, but if you can go into a daze, you can enter Theta.

Theta

As I mentioned before, the Theta brainwave state is the

state we enter during daydreaming, hypnosis, meditation and dreaming. A little known fact is that this state is contagious. If you are able to enter the Theta state, you will quite likely be able to bring others into the state as well, provided the right conditions are in place.

If you meditate frequently, it is quite likely that you are very familiar with this state and can enter it at will. If not, I'd like to share my video series on how to achieve the Theta state. It is located in the digital bonus material. There are also written instructions on the next few pages.

Benefits of being able to enter the Theta state:

- Silence mental chatter

- Improve mental clarity

- Sleep more deeply and peacefully

- Remain calm even under pressure

- Reach increased levels of relaxation

- Clear out the extra mind-garbage to make way for inner guidance and wisdom

- Great for meditation and everyday use- imagine walking through life in a state of peace

63

- Experience being in the NOW

- Greatly reduce stress

- Improve relationships

- Build and access intuition

- Observe life rather than be overwhelmed by it

- Improve every aspect of health- mentally, physically and emotionally

- Connect with the divine

- Guide your clients into this deeper state in order for them to be able to more deeply receive

Using the Theta state to consciously meditate is highly beneficial. When meditating, you are merely slowing down your brainwaves. This slower brainwave state puts you in touch with more of yourself on far deeper levels than you are usually able to access. Slowing your brainwaves down is meant to quiet and soothe your left-brain and ego. Ego and the left-brain are often the troublemakers of the mind- creating feelings of lack and worry. So, quieting your mind is really about quieting the parts of the brain that we usually function under. In meditation, you are getting in touch with parts of yourself and your mind that you normally don't have access to. This downshift allows your creative right-brain and subconscious to communicate with you. The Theta state is the gateway to the intuitive mind. So if you are interested in developing your intuition or communicating with the Divine, this is a very important state to be able achieve, as well.

You may find that your mind isn't quiet at all when you first begin to meditate. Parts of you have been waiting a long time for you to slow down enough to notice and hear them. It is likely you may be suddenly inspired while in this state because more of you is activated and answers seem to simply appear, effortlessly. As a fantastic side effect, this state also brings a physical sense of peace and well-being most of us almost never experience.

Entering Theta

- Don't force anything. This is about letting it happen rather than making it happen. Surrender.
- Practice makes perfect. You may not get these

techniques right the first time. Keep trying them until you begin to feel heavy, relaxed, sleepy, dazed, or waves of swirling energy.

- These techniques are varied & meant to work for different people with diverse learning styles. Don't get frustrated if one doesn't work for you.

- If you have trouble entering Theta, you can try asking your higher self or a divine being of your choice to go in with you. For unknown reasons, it is easier to enter with others than by yourself.

- Don't tell your brain to be quiet. It's okay to let your mind wander, you may get the wisest guidance or epiphanies if you just go with the flow.

- The various parts of your brain and the Divine have been waiting to tell you things, so your mind will be extra busy at first. Take notes if you'd like. A quiet mind will come eventually with time and practice.

- Method #1: Sit quietly- with your eyes closed at first; though you may work your way up to open eyes if desired. Picture, imagine or feel a hoop floating above your head. Allow/observe this hoop beginning to move downward at its own pace. Don't try to force it. If it hovers somewhere, it's likely healing that area. For some this may not look like a hoop. It may seem like a dome lowering over you, a ball of light riding a slinky or spiral downward, a tornado around you and so on. Be aware that it may not be visual at all for you, it may seem like you're imagining or perceiving a hoop rather than getting a visual picture in your mind's eye. Once it gets to your feet, it will likely begin making its way back up. The speed will vary from person to person, depending on how well your energy is currently flowing. It's not necessary to stay with this visualization once you feel relaxed and droopy. The whole point is to get into the zone. What you choose to do while you're in the zone is up to you.*

- Method #2: Begin by using this technique in a fairly quiet atmosphere, then work your way up to noisy surroundings. Sit quietly- with your eyes closed at first; work your way up to open eyes if desired. Listen for the silence beneath all sound. Consider this: If your surroundings were completely silent that's what you would hear. This silence is still present even when sound is occurring; it's just below the sound. When I use this technique I often imagine I'm in an elevator being lowered down through all of the sounds into the silence. It's not about ignoring the other sounds, it is being aware of the silence even though there are sounds.*

- Method #3: Sit quietly with your eyes open. Find an object about the size of a quarter at least 3 feet away from you. Gaze at this object, while also seeing everything in your peripheral vision. Allow your gaze to soften and relax, like when you used to daydream in class as a kid. If you find your eyes beginning to hurt or burn, you can close them once you've gotten into the zone. You may want to practice opening and closing them to see if you can stay in.*

- Going Deeper: Once you've discovered which method works best for you, go into Theta as best you can, then ask your brain to take you deeper, then deeper, then as deep as you can go for your highest good. Play with the levels you can reach by instructing your brain to take you higher or lower.

- When you're finished, make sure to ground yourself using the grounding technique. You may even want to combine these methods with grounding or sending Essence energy. It feels even more blissful, plus helps you tap into information more easily.

Once you're in the Theta brainwave state, you are tapped in to way more than usual. Pay attention to your thoughts while in the zone. Remember that it quiets your ego & left-brain so that your whole self can come through. The top question I get when teaching people how to develop their intuition is how they can be sure it's true guidance and not just imagination. It just boils down to experience and practice. I highly recommend finding a buddy who has similar interests that you can call up and share your findings with. Practicing together can be helpful as well, because we often amplify each other's abilities. It is vital to have someone you can exchange information with or check in with when you're first learning to tap in to divine guidance; it helps you build trust in the information you receive, as well as learning how to differentiate between guidance and imagination or even ego.

Learning Styles

You may already be accessing your intuition without even knowing it. I took a psychic development class in the 90's and came out of it feeling completely in the dark. It put me off the metaphysical track for another 10 years. All because the teacher was clairvoyant and was attempting to teach clairvoyance. Unfortunately, that isn't everyone's gift.

There are various forms of psychic abilities. Clairvoyance is the ability to see colors, lights, images, and to have visions. Clairaudience allows you to hear messages from beyond as well as cosmic sounds within your mind through psychic hearing. Clairsentience gives you the ability to have sudden flashes of understanding and inner knowing of whole concepts and ideas. Clairgustance is getting intuitive information through your sense of taste. Clairsalience is the gift of smelling intuitively. Empathic abilities allow you to feel the emotions and sensations of others.

Depending on our learning styles and the way we interact with the world, each of us will have different abilities. If you're visual and tend to think in pictures, you will likely be clairvoyant. If you are highly tuned into your body, you will most likely have Empathic abilities. If you tend to think in words, you may be clairsentient. If you are highly tuned in to auditory things or have sensitive hearing, you may be clairaudient. I'm sure you get the picture.

Most of us have one of these as our primary gift, but with patience and practice can often develop some of the other abilities as well to varying degrees. It is very important that you let go of any expectations of what your intuition should look like and work with what you've got. The trick is to discover your current strongest ability and focus on building those skills. Over time, the others will begin to appear. It also helps to raise your vibration and keep your energy as unobstructed as possible through grounding, meditation and energy healing. If you would like more information on the different types of intuition, you can check out the book *You Are Psychic!* by Peter Sanders.

Clairvoyance is the most recognized and sought after

ability, but also the most rare because most people think in words, not pictures. Empathy is the most common but least recognized. The other abilities generally fall somewhere in between. You can go to any major bookseller and find myriad books on clairvoyance, but only a handful on other abilities. As our culture is currently awakening, I am seeing changes in this dynamic lately. More and more information is coming to light as an increased number of people tap into their inner guidance. At the end of this chapter, I will share the information I've compiled on Empathic abilities, as that is my own primary ability and I had to search for information as I was "waking up."

Another piece of information you need to understand in order to make the most of your intuition is that each individual thing or situation has its own unique vibrational frequency. Everything from a toothache to a heart attack to a break-up has a distinctive resonance all its own because it is all energy. When we are focused on or are experiencing something, it is in our energy field/aura. Anyone who is sensitive to energy can pick up those vibrations. It is then up to their brains to translate these frequencies into information the person can understand. This is all done subconsciously.

Let's say one of your coworkers has a toothache. If you were clairvoyant you might keep seeing visuals of a dentist, a tooth, a person holding their face in pain, or something visual that represents tooth pain in your perception. However, if you are an Empath, you might feel your own tooth hurting. If clairaudient, you might hear a dentist's drill or painful moaning. A clairsentient may think "Ask about their tooth" or remember a time they had a tooth problem. In order for these reactions to be intuitive, of course, the coworker would be showing no outward signs of tooth pain and you would have no prior conscious knowledge of the toothache. Otherwise these reactions are just run of the mill empathy and/or sympathy.

Protection

The level to which you experience the above phenomenon often depends on your level of sensitivity as well as your level of connection to the person you're picking up on. It can happen from being physically near someone, thinking about them, talking to them on the phone, texting them, emailing them, or intending to energetically tune into them. As you can imagine, sometimes this is unintentional. If you would like to have your own body & mind back, rather than feeling someone else's experience, the grounding exercise in Chapter One is a big help. If your vibration is high, lower vibrational things will be deflected.

Pay attention to sudden things you pick up out of the blue that you weren't experiencing before. This will help you establish what belongs to you and what doesn't. This is most difficult for an Empath, but all intuitives struggle with some level of this. You must consciously acknowledge and release the symptom/issue as not belonging to you. You may send love energy to whomever it belongs to, but let the issue go yourself. It will not help the person with the issue if you take their struggles on yourself. They signed up for that experience on a spirit level, so you are not only robbing them of their own journey, you are depleting yourself. Better to blast energy that can be replenished than to allow other people's stuff to bog you down.

The most important thing you must remember while developing your intuition is patience. It takes practice,

practice, and more practice to recognize and develop these skills. Don't be frustrated or shy about getting as much experience and feedback as possible.

Intuition Attunement

Just as any healing modality has activations or attunements, so do various abilities. You can sit quietly in meditation and ask your higher self or your guides for your intuitive abilities to be activated, and then just observe your experience, with whichever sense is most dominant for you, for a few minutes. An attunement will clear blockages and open your energetic channel to receive divine messages more clearly. Yes, you will still have to go through the energetic cleansing process mentioned in the attunement section in Chapter Seven just like with energy healing attunements.

Getting Answers

The top priority for most people who desire intuitive abilities is getting answers and guidance from their guides & spirit as to their next step in life. Guides are spirits/energy beings who have remained in energy form, rather than choosing to live a physical lifetime. They are specially assigned to work with individuals who are in physical form in order to help guide them from a higher perspective. Your guide or guides are actually your peers. They are no higher or lower than you in rank or divinity. Their sole purpose is to help you out, so never hesitate to contact them.

The first thing you want to do is ground, and go into Theta. Call in your guides to assist. Your intention is what's important here. So whatever wording you'd like to use is fine, while intending for your guide or guides to surround you- both for protection and to make sure the information you receive is divine. When tuning in to the ethers, the possibility always exists that discarnate entities (spirits who haven't gone into the light, but are not alive in a physical body either) can hijack the session. Calling in your guides ensures a more pure connection than just randomly calling out for information. Discarnate spirits are often misguided and looking out for their own interests. Don't be afraid, it is not as bad as Hollywood makes it seem. You just want to go straight to the source, by specifically calling in whichever divine beings you wish to converse with. Your guides, your Essence/Higher Self, God/Source, Jesus, Buddha, and certain angels are all good examples of pure information sources. Having your guides stand guard is always a good idea.

If you'd like to know who you are conversing with in each session, you can pick a few of your favorite divine beings and call them forth with your intention- either silently or out loud- individually. With each one, ask them to show you your signal that represents your connection with that particular being. Depending on your intuitive ability, this may be a physical sensation, a visual cue- such as a color, light, or spark, or even an image of that being, a sound in your inner hearing, a taste or a smell- just observe what happens when you ask for the signal. Repeat this process a few times until you're clear on the signal. Now you know when you're tuned in to that particular energy.

Once you've established your signals, you can call in

whomever you'd like information from. The first order of business is getting your signals for yes and no answers. Ask to be shown your signal for yes. Sit quietly and observe all of your senses. Repeat this process until you're clear on the signal that keeps coming to you. Be aware that this signal may be quite subtle at first, so pay attention to even the tiniest sensations or visuals you perceive. My initial 'yes' was a swirling of energy in my stomach/solar plexus area. Repeat this process for a 'no' signal. My personal 'no' was my tongue feeling numb. If you don't immediately have any signals jumping out at you, you can just sit with your questions and feel into your body. Joy, peace, giddiness and good feelings are a simple 'yes.' Heaviness, dread, pain and negative feelings are telling you 'no.'

Yet another simple method of getting answers is sway testing. Stand with your feet planted, hips width apart. Close your eyes and ask your yes or no question. If you begin to feel yourself falling forward, it's a yes. If you begin to tip backward, it is a no. You can also do this with food, supplements and other things you're not sure about. Hold the item out in front of you, at arms length. If you sway toward it, it would be be beneficial for you. If you sway away from it, it would not.

Once you have your personal signals in place, you can begin asking questions such as "Is it for my highest good to do this?" or "Would I be pleased with the results if I did this?" Do not ask, "Should I do this?" We have free will in our human journey and they will not give clear answers to such inquiries, since it's ultimately up to us.

You may begin to find other confirmation signals creeping in as you pay more attention and begin looking for answers. Have you ever been listening to a beautiful singer and broken out in chills? This is your soul saying yes. Pay attention to this and use it as a truth meter. It will happen more and more over time as you practice and acknowledge it. Other common confirmations are seeing a spark with eyes open or closed, feeling a tapping or tingling on top of your head, pressure in the middle of your forehead (third eye activating) or a tightening in the abdomen. These are just a few, but there are many ways to get confirmation on things.

The best possible way to get answers is to follow your emotions. If you feel drawn to, excited by, or passionate about something, it's for you. Do you feel giddy or entranced by something? Follow that feeling! Alternately if you feel tense, sad, heavy, anxious, fearful or angry, walk away. Our emotions can be reacting to our own thoughts, a person we're interacting with or a situation set before us. Our emotions show us what resonates with our true selves (Essences) and what doesn't. We've been entrained to ignore our emotions, but they are meant to be a compass for us. For more information on this concept and techniques to try, check out the book *The Astonishing Power of Emotions* by Esther and Jerry Hicks.

Releasing Entities

Many people freak out when this topic is raised. There are sometimes spirits of people who have died that have not yet gone into the light. This means that their energy remains on the Earth plane. Don't let Hollywood freak you out about this. It is not like you see in the movies. When we die, we turn into pure energy and consciousness. When we go into the light, we receive a healing and rebalancing, as well as the knowledge of who we truly are and all of the lifetimes we've had and everything in between. If we haven't gone into the light, we remain nearly as confused and limited as we are in physical bodies. Hauntings and possessions are simply those confused beings attaching themselves to places or people. These things do occur. They just don't happen to the extent that we've seen portrayed in the media.

When a spirit remains on the Earth plane, it is usually for one or more of the following reasons:

- They don't realize they're deceased yet.
- They feel they have some kind of unfinished business here.
- They were told they were going to Hell if they did certain things, and they've done those things - so they're afraid going into the light means going to Hell.
- They want to remain close to someone who is still alive.
- They're just plain stubborn.

In order to release these beings, you have to first be able to recognize that they're there. I suggest asking your guides to show you your signal for discarnate spirits/entities.

This would be accomplished by using the same method as getting your 'yes' and 'no' signals. My personal entity signal is feeling like a cold or electric finger is lightly touching or tapping me anywhere from the neck down. The same feeling from the neck up is Divine beings that live in the light. Your signal may be this or something else. Take your time on getting clear on your own signal.

When you've established that there is an entity or energy that needs to cross over, all you have to do is have a conversation with them. This can be in your mind or out loud. I usually do this silently. Calmly explain that they are deceased and let them know they can go into the light. If you still feel they haven't left, you can tell them that Hell simply doesn't exist. It was a scare tactic invented by people to control other people. Ask the Divine beings around you to show them the truth of who and what they are. Discuss the fact that when they go, all that happens is a reunion with their soul family and a greater understanding of their journey from a higher perspective. If that doesn't do the trick, let them know that any unfinished business can still be dealt with from beyond the light and that they can visit loved ones in energy anytime they want to.

If all else fails, you can call in the being's soul family to escort them into the light. This usually works quite well. I've only ever had one occasion where this process didn't work. I had a client on my table for a session and I felt a male energy attached to her. I performed the entire process listed above and he still remained. I gathered up all of my empowered energy and said "If you won't go into the light, then you must leave us. You are not welcome within me or my client or this space ever again. Go now." I felt him leave and saw, in my mind's eye, him walking down the stairwell. Without knowing why (I was channeling this) I said "Wait." Then "I want you to know that you can call your soul family forth any time you change your mind and they will bring you into the light. It is your choice and your free will. I wish you peace." In that moment, there was a flash of light and he went. Sometimes the stubborn ones need to know that it's their choice.

When a being goes into the light, I generally feel the energy in the room shift from lower to higher vibration (heavy energy becomes lighter.) I will also usually have some kind of perception of energy flowing upward and to the left. Pay attention to what you witness occurring as you practice this. In my experience, finding spirits to release is something that you may only experience occasionally at first- almost as though you're going through a training period. Eventually it can happen more often and at times when you're not really expecting it, but for most, this doesn't occur until you're ready.

When someone has a spirit attached to them, it is common for them to feel drained or moody for no apparent reason. This is generally the extent of the effects. There are rare occasions where these spirits can create stronger effects but it is exceedingly uncommon. The people most likely to have such attachments are chronic people pleasers. If you are constantly allowing others to use you up and control you, you are likely to be giving that permission to spirits and people alike, on an unconscious level. You want so badly to help others, that you're willing to give them your own energy. This does not actually help anyone. It's time to stand up and say ENOUGH! It is important to know that spirits have to leave if you tell them to. You absolutely have the power and ability to do this.

One more related topic I'd like to cover is the concept of evil or demons. This is something that the metaphysical community is fairly divided on. It has been my experience that if you expect evil, you get it. Early strict Christian programming will often create a belief in Satan, evil and demons. There will commonly be a deeply ingrained belief that getting in touch with any of this will open a gateway to such evil. Your subconscious mind can create danger where it doesn't actually exist. If you feel that this is a concern for you, I would suggest that you use the process described in Chapter Twelve to let go of any programs that keep you believing in evil and fearing your natural abilities.

The Screen

Now let's explore the next level of intuitive development. I'm sure you've enjoyed playing with getting yesses and nos. After a while, that's not enough anymore. At some point, most people want clearer answers and information. Plus yes and no answers can only get you so far. Much of the world is not black or white, so I'm going to show you how to access those shades of gray.

Once again, ground, enter Theta, call in your guides and sit quietly. Envision a blank screen in front of you, as though you are in a movie theatre. If you are visual, this may be quite easy for you. If you are not visual, there are other options. First, you can imagine or perceive a blank screen. For example, if I said, "picture an elephant", what would you "see"? Some would get a clear visual of an elephant, some would just think of a trunk while others may perceive the bulk of an elephant within their mind, but not get any clear visuals on it. This blank screen is meant to create a void in order for things to begin to come through unobstructed. It doesn't matter how clearly you envision it; it only serves to clear your mental slate.

Now that you have your screen in whatever way you can imagine it, ask a question and wait. Don't try to make anything happen. Just allow whatever happens. Pay attention to all of your senses. What are you seeing, imagining, perceiving, thinking about, feeling, smelling, hearing, tasting? If you get anything, think about what that represents to you. Trust that WHATEVER comes through is part of your answer. Yes, even your thought streams. Let your mind wander. When you're first starting out, keep repeating this process until you get anything at all, and then once you've had more practice and experience, you will find that your full query will be answered. Whether you like the answer, or not, is an entirely different matter.

Don't worry if all you get in the beginning are feelings in your body or seemingly normal thought streams. Just allow your abilities to show themselves in whatever way comes more naturally. You will begin to develop more diverse abilities the more you practice and energetically open. When you feel ready, you can begin trying this on others by tuning into them and following the same process.

Dreams

Our dreams are an especially easy place to get intuitive messages and visitations from beyond. Dreams that are extremely vivid and memorable usually have a message attached. Keeping a journal next to your bed and jotting down the highlights of your dreams conveys to your mind and the Universe that you are ready to receive messages in that way. Make sure to write things down the moment you wake up. Those dreams can be slippery! Know that it will take practice to begin regularly remembering dreams and interpreting the messages.

I believe that if a deceased loved one visits you in a dream that they are actually visiting you. It is also often a signal that you are about to embark on discovering your Mediumship abilities. Guides will often introduce themselves in dreams as well. The dream state is Theta, so you are very open and receptive while dreaming. It's not surprising that we often get some interesting messages, releases and visitations as we dream.

There is another aspect of dreaming called lucid dreaming. This is where you become conscious that you are dreaming, but remain asleep and dreaming. In this state, you can usually control the dream, rather than just helplessly watching it unfold. You can practice lucid dreaming by lying down & allowing your whole body to relax. You can use a Theta method to get you into the zone, but the point is to go all floppy and relaxed, but not to let yourself fall asleep. If you experience any itches during the relaxation phase ignore them. Then just watch the thoughts and images that begin to play in your head, as you remain fully relaxed. Play with controlling what you see and feel. Eventually you should be able to control all of your dreams. This is not as easy as it sounds. For most, it takes years to master, though for a lucky few it's a natural ability.

Be aware that lucid dreaming sometimes brings you into a state called sleep paralysis. This is where your mind is alert and aware but your body is so relaxed it feels like you couldn't move if you tried. I'd like to reassure you that you can move. It just feels like you can't. If you try and are unable, simply count yourself up to full consciousness intending to be fully awake and mobile by the time you get to 10. For most, none of this is a concern because it is common to eventually fall asleep during a lucid dream practice. Set an alarm if you try it in the middle of the day.

Auras

Seeing auras, the field of energy around objects and people, is one of the things people tend to strive for while developing their abilities. I want to stress that it is far more likely for naturally clairvoyant people to see auras in color-especially at first. But it is possible for anyone to see the energy field to some extent.

The best place to begin seeing auras is outdoors. I recommend trees as your first viewing subjects. Pick a day with a beautiful blue sky. Find a spot with trees around where the sun isn't in your direct line of sight, but the sky is. Relax, get into Theta if you can, and gaze just above the tree or trees for a while. You may begin to see something fuzzy like static in the sky. Congratulations, you're now able to see the molecules of the air and the flow of energy movement. This alone is a significant feat. For most beginners, auras will usually look like smoke, fog, denser collections of staticy looking molecules, or faint color. It will likely be very slight at first. This is fine, as you're just beginning to build this skill. The more you practice, the better you'll be able to see.

There is an optical illusion aspect to seeing auras that you should beware of. If you gaze at anything for a long period of time, your eyes create an image like the negative of a photo, so if you look an inch or two higher, the edge of the object will have a shadow around it that your eyes are creating. This is not an aura, just your eyes adjusting to a new focus.

When you feel ready to begin trying this on humans, you can either go to the beach and practice the tree technique on people about 20-30 feet away, or you can find someone willing to be your practice dummy. If you have a partner for aura viewing practice, I suggest finding a space that has multiple choices for wall colorings behind you. Traditional books on viewing auras will tell you to choose a white background, which is great if you are able to see color, but most beginners cannot. Try as many different backgrounds as you can-white, black, blue, brown, smooth, rough, light, dark and patterned backgrounds. You can also play with various lighting options- just don't do it with light or sun shining into your eyes. Play with all of the different situations you can in order to determine what allows you to see energy best; it is different for everyone.

Sit or stand about 10-15 feet in front of the person, relax, go into Theta/daydream state and gaze at the empty space about 3 inches above their head. You're not looking at the wall; you're focused on the space not the physical. Just let yourself relax totally and see what happens. Sometimes you'll see the smoky movement of their aura, sometimes you'll see the person begin to look different- as though you're seeing more deeply into them or a different version of them. Just go with whatever happens. The more you do these techniques, the more effective they will become. Don't be afraid to keep trying different backgrounds as you develop, since your abilities will constantly be evolving. What was once a challenge could become your favorite method once you've had more experience.

People who are especially good at seeing the aura will sometimes offer aura readings. This is done by tuning into the aura and examining where it flows well, where there are dark or stagnant spots, what colors they observe and so on. This helps them understand more about the person and what they need to work on. There are also special photography instruments that can take pictures of the aura. If reading the aura is something you're interested in, the Internet is full of information on what the colors mean and so on. The colors of the aura are often directly correlated to the chakra colors and their meanings.

Building Trust

When you first begin working on these skills, it's normal to doubt the information coming through. It often seems like you're just making up or imagining things, especially since everything is filtered, deciphered and translated by your brain. Everything you get will appear to be coming from you. This is part of the reason that being in Theta is so important- your brain is accessing different things than it normally does and you can trust the process from this state more easily.

Adopting the buddy system with skill building is essential. Find someone who is equally interested in intuition and check in with them on whether they get any sort of confirmation from your experiences. You can also practice these techniques on each other, once you get comfortable playing with your intuition. Make sure you pair up with someone you feel comfortable with, so you can put anything out there. Keep in mind that even experienced psychics are only able to have their information confirmed about 80% of the time. The less you hold back, the more you can grow.

Here are some ideas for finding a buddy if you don't already have someone in mind. Look at your pool of friends. Is there anyone you feel comfortable talking about metaphysical topics with? Ask them if you can tune into them to practice intuitive skills. Have them tell you when you're correct as well as when they get chills. Check out meetup.com; this is a free website where you can find groups in the area with similar interests. Chances are there will be a metaphysical group or a psychic development class in your area. If you begin attending some of these groups, you may bond with someone and find your partner. Another possibility is contacting your local metaphysical shop, psychic or Reiki practitioner for suggestions. Lastly, I am available for sessions through Skype, FaceTime, or in person if you'd like to work with me privately.

Channeling

It is my firm belief that everyone is capable of channeling. Once again it boils down to confidence, trust and practice. Channeling is the process of contacting divine beings and bringing through messages to guide yourself and others. This is done by grounding, sitting quietly, going into Theta, calling in your guides and asking them either a specific question, or intending to bring through a message for the highest good of whomever you're tuning in to. After that, you just wait for words to pop into your head and either say them or write them down. Sometimes it will be a word at a time, other times it may be a whole sentence at once or even an entire concept. It is up to you to just speak the words or describe the concept.

Most people I teach this to get nervous right about now. We've been taught that only the most connected people can channel. Trust me, you are just as connected as anyone else. Perhaps this will ease your mind- I'm not asking you to start out by doing this in front of anyone. What I recommend is to either write down the words that come into your mind or record them somewhere that only you will hear (most smart phones have a recorder app), then listen to or read the message once you feel you've gotten all that you're going to get.

When I first began attempting to channel messages, all I would get is "love, love, love, love..." or "meditate,

meditate, meditate, meditate..." Eventually I started receiving lengthier messages- especially once I was getting into Theta more easily. In the beginning they all began with "You are living a life of..." or "She is living a life of..." That's how I knew they had begun. This was at a time when I usually didn't trust myself enough to speak them out loud yet. I would be in a Reiki session and silently ask if there were any messages for that person, listen to the message in my head and mention the general synopsis of the channel to them at the end of their session. Once I'd had enough confirmation that the messages made sense to people, I began channeling out loud at the beginning of most sessions, after calling in their guides and other divine helpers. People often find great value and peace in the messages brought through for them.

One last thought, make sure you know who you're channeling. You can use the signals you've developed to know who you're conversing with on your own behalf, but with others it's different because you don't have signals set up with their divine helpers. The best insurance policy is to call in their divine guides & helpers before starting the channel. Ask them to protect & guide you both as you bring through a message for their highest good. Don't just sit down and randomly ask for a message without bringing in the Help. This only opens you both up for energetic attachments and false messages. Don't be too overly concerned with this though. These precautions will be all you need to safely and successfully channel. If all else fails, there are always the techniques to release entities discussed earlier in this chapter.

Mediumship

Before beginning any level of mediumship work, I'd like to clarify how I perceive talking to spirits or ghosts. Most of us start out thinking of mediumship in the way Hollywood presents it to us, so it seems extra hokey, not to mention frightening. I've mentioned before that we, as humans, carry all of our stuff around in our energy fields and the more sensitive among us can pick up on that. When we die, we return to pure energy and consciousness (or Essence.) In that form, we still carry the memories and feelings from each lifetime within our energy. Sensitive people can also pick up on that. It's just like reading someone who's alive, minus the body. However, it's nothing like the movies- that's what usually trips us up.

Mediums are simply channelers for loved ones who have crossed over. Essentially, if you can channel, you can build mediumship skills. This means everyone. Including you- if you want to. However, there is another aspect to mediumship because bringing through messages is only half of the job. While doing this kind of work, you may also come across spirits who have not crossed over yet. Normally these beings come to sensitive people because they want someone who can interact with them- in essence, they are looking for someone to assist them to cross over, whether they know it or not. If you decide to develop these skills, make sure you are comfortable with the discarnate entity release process.

Begin by grounding, entering the Theta state, calling in your guides and the guides of whomever you'd like to read for, intending for them to protect and guide you both. Call in any loved ones who wish to communicate with the subject of your reading. You can ask for specific loved ones, but most of the time, the spirits choose who comes forward, rather than us. Ask the person you're reading for to only say yes or no to things you say while you're practicing. You don't want them giving away the story & putting thoughts into your head. You can ask them for the whole story once you've finished the reading. Take your time tuning into whomever shows up. Remain grounded and in high vibration. Don't force anything- just observe whatever is there. Which side of the person is the spirit standing on? What are you feeling? What is popping into your head? What do you perceive seeing, thinking, hearing, smelling, tasting? Describe each thing as it comes up. Don't hold anything back. Silently ask what gender they are and say whatever comes to you. Ask what they're wearing, if they have an object for the person to relate to, their age and any other questions you can think of. Share whatever comes through as you get it.

There are trickier things you can ask, like their name, which is a difficult thing to bring through for most people. Chances are if you're uncertain about the name it's not right on, but if it comes through with a level of confidence you've got it. If you bring a piece of information through and it doesn't mean anything to the person, just skip to the next thing. Sometimes the person you're reading for just doesn't know or remember that detail. Another interesting question to ask is how they died. As usual, the answer can come in through multiple senses. Pay attention to your body & if you have sudden pain somewhere. See if any words, pictures or concepts come through. Mention whatever you experience. Finally, ask if they have a message for the person and as with channeling, say whatever words and ideas pop into your head.

A more advanced technique that you can work up to is allowing the spirit to merge with you for the period of the reading. Only do this if you feel confident that they have already gone into the light, and you are empowered enough to fully take back your energy field afterward. When you allow them to merge with you, you can momentarily get a stronger sense of their energy, who they were and maybe even a closer look at their appearance. This all allows you to bring their energy and description alive for the recipient of the reading. Afterward, you just intend that your Essence move fully back into your body & that your body solely belongs to you. You can also envision closing your chakras as though they have eyelids. This allows them to continue functioning, but lets go of anything that belongs to anyone else.

If you feel uneasy in some way while communicating with a spirit, ask whether they have gone into the light yet. If not, it's time to utilize your entity releasing skills from earlier in this chapter. Be patient with yourself. There was a five year span between finding out I was an Empath and developing enough confidence and skill to learn mediumship. Developing intuition is a constantly evolving process that you have to keep working on, probably for the rest of your life. There is no end to the knowledge available to us, if we just continue seeking.

Empaths

Most people have some level of empathic ability. I have my own personal theory as to how it develops more strongly in some than others. In my experience, the most sensitive Empaths grew up with someone who was mentally or emotionally unstable. This can range from a hot temper or deep depression up to schizophrenia and everything in between. When we are young and in an unstable environment, we develop our own protective mechanisms. In this case, subconsciously sending out our energy to feel out the person in question.

Let's say you have an abusive father. There are likely times that it is safe to be around him but others that it isn't. By energetically tuning into him, you find out, in your own body through feelings, whether it's safe or not. If you feel agitated around him you can avoid him or behave extra well in his presence so as not to incur his wrath. This becomes such a great tool for you that you eventually begin to use this method of energetically checking everyone out. Constantly. I feel that the level to which this gift develops is dependent on the intensity of the situation you grew up with.

The same principal can be applied to other psychic abilities, but with empathy, you begin to believe everything you're picking up on in others actually belongs to you. Earlier I used the example of a coworker with a toothache. Using the same example, an Empath may pick up the toothache and believe it's their own tooth that hurts. They may even go as far as to make a dentist appointment, only to have the dentist tell them there's nothing wrong with the tooth. A clairvoyant wouldn't keep picturing a tooth all day and think it was their own issue, nor would any of the other types of psychic take someone else's issue and make it their own.

In this way, Empaths tend to suffer much more than any other intuitive person. They move through the world feeling the issues and pain of others without even knowing it. Empaths will often be reclusive, phobic of public places, or even be considered hypochondriacs. They also tend to be found in the more nurturing industries such as nursing, mothering, counseling and healing. It is their goal to take care of others in order to make themselves feel better, because they only feel good if the people around them feel good.

Are you wondering if you're an Empath? Do you suddenly have anxiety when you're near someone who is stressed? Do you have a hard time going to the mall or grocery store because it drains you completely? Do you feel that it's your responsibility to make everyone else happy? Are you always trying to take care of everyone? Do you need to be alone in order to recharge your batteries? Do you encounter various mystery symptoms that make no sense as you go about your day? If you answered yes to more than one of these questions, you are quite likely an Empath.

Don't worry, there's help for you yet. My favorite method of protection against empathic overwhelm is the grounding technique combined with imagining my energy field pulling in closer to my body & telling it to mind its own business. This will take a lot of practice and you may have to do it several times throughout the day, but it can eventually become your natural state. Whenever you're feeling off, give this a try and see if it changes how you feel. If you'd like more information on being empathic, check out the book *Whose Stuff is This?* by Yvonne Perry. She was an extreme case and was one of the first to bring the topic of Empaths to light by writing an informative book on the topic. She offers other methods of protection as well, but in my experience, blasting your own high vibration energy is the best protection you can get without having to close yourself off in any way. Closing yourself off can keep you from receiving good stuff as well as bad. As always, trust your gut for finding the method that works best for you. You may even find that just knowing what's happening to you helps ease things in your life.

*The three methods or portals into the Theta state are from a modality called Presence, which was created by Reinier Bosman. More information can be found on www.Presence4Life.com. I am certified as a Presence trainer.

Chapter Seven

From Reiki to Essence

I was fortunate enough to be blessed with a Reiki teacher who taught us to follow our intuition in our healing work. We were given the basics of traditional Usui Reiki, but very much encouraged to do what felt right to us. This spoke to me immediately because I had always been turned off to traditionalism, especially in spiritual matters. It never made sense to me that I had to go to a specific building, follow certain rules and speak particular words in order to connect with the Divine. While I certainly started with the bones of traditional Reiki, it didn't take me long to begin letting it evolve to suit my clients and myself. Many of my clients can attest to the fact that this has created a powerful energy session, far more tangible than much of the energy work available out there.

Essence Healing has been, in part, inspired by the work of Esther Hicks- the channel for Abraham, who originally introduced the concept of the Law of Attraction. I had already been getting the message that we need to ground our spirits into our physical bodies more at this time. I was also channeling that our feelings were meant to be a compass for us & that we needed to reconnect with those feelings. I've recently seen many people, including myself, have major catalysts show up in our lives that reset us back to our original emotional sensitivity. Just as I was noticing all of this, I kept having Ester Hicks show up in my consciousness and everywhere else- Facebook, the bookstore, Amazon, clients mentioning her and so on. I woke up one morning feeling that there was something I was supposed to be reading and Hicks popped into my head right away. I went onto Facebook to see if she had anything new to promote and guess who was at the top of my newsfeed? Esther Hicks. I said, "Well played, Universe. Well played."

In my search I found a book called *The Astonishing Power of Emotions: Let Your Feelings be Your Guide*. Oddly enough, all of my recent channels had been about exactly that, so I knew I was on the right track. I read the book and resonated so strongly with its message. Primarily the piece that the Universe wanted me to pick up was that we need to vibrationally resonate with our higher selves. It's not enough to set intentions. It's not enough to ground. It's not enough to pay attention to our feelings. We must combine those things while raising our vibration to meet that of our Essence. I highly recommend the book if you would like more information on this concept, as I can hardly do it justice here. However, The Essence Healing System will teach you how to do all of these things and more- combining my own most powerful healing methods with the very essence of your being in order to create greater peace, wisdom, healing, balance, joy, empowerment and grace in yourself and those around you, whether you use it in your everyday life or in a healing practice.

Why Essence Healing?

If you've seen one healing modality you've seen them all, right? Not necessarily. As I began practicing the Essence Healing modality on people I noticed that their feedback was different. They were coming out of sessions feeling high, as though they had been given some fantastic drug with no negative side effects. Floaty feelings, out of body experiences, interdimensional travel, overwhelming peace, extreme lightness or a weighted feeling were among the experiences they shared. One especially hilarious client said "There's not a joint you could roll that would make me feel as good as your sessions do." I knew, right away, that I couldn't keep this technique to myself.

I'd like to suggest that what sets this healing method apart from others is the deep connection with the truer self it initiates and builds. It is not just a healing modality. If you can stick with it for just a few weeks, it can become a whole new lifestyle of peace and balance for every aspect of your life. The other characteristic that sets it apart is the recognition and acceptance of your own power, your own God-Self.

The difference between most healing modalities and Essence Healing is that you're no longer just the physical channel for the energy of the universe/divine. You are the SOURCE of the energy. Think of it as being the sun as opposed to a laser beam. The God spark within you- whatever you choose to call it- is a never-ending source of healing, wisdom, energy and power. Your physical self may experience limitation on a regular basis, but your spirit, your Essence, is part of the Source of All That Is, and is, therefore, limitless. When coupled with your body, this becomes an unstoppable force.

Even if you don't ever plan to become a professional energy worker, this book and the methods you learn within it can transform your life for the better. It takes practice and focus, but once you've made it a priority the benefits are endless. Imagine feeling emotionally balanced and confident. Think about how empowering it would be to heal your own body and mind, while effortlessly raising the vibration of everyone and everything you encounter. This is all part of Essence Healing.

Healing with your entire being is empowering and beyond what we had previously been able to experience in the physical form. Of course you can boost this healing by involving the Universe and the Divine as well. You can combine this modality with any other you'd like. I highly encourage experimentation and the use of intuition. A true healer relies far more heavily on the intuitive guidance they receive from within, than the protocol of any healing modality. The instructions for utilizing your own healing abilities are already within you. This book is simply a tool to help you unlock them.

I want to be clear that this healing system is not about giving away your own energy or taking the energy of others into you to be healed. Both of those methods will deplete you quickly. The techniques and concepts you will learn here will boost and invigorate you, and, quite likely, bliss you out. When you ground your Essence into your body, you become the perfect marriage of Earth and Divine. Your connection to both will constantly refill and restore you if you intend and allow it. Using this energy to heal is far more powerful, healthy and empowering than sharing your own life force energy.

My wish for you, above all else, is that you become unquestioningly empowered and confident in your ability to raise your energetic vibration and that of those around you in ways that will begin to change lives as well as the world. You are capable of this; there is no question in my mind. The only thing holding you back is you and the programming you've received while living on Earth. I'm here to tell you that it is possible to navigate your way back to whom you were meant to be.

Asking for Permission

One of the questions commonly asked when people are learning any format of energy healing is whether we need to ask permission before sending healing energy to someone. There are two schools of thought on this. First, any traditional Reiki teacher will tell you to absolutely ask first. Sometimes a practitioner will go as far as to ask before working on someone who has specifically come to their office seeking energy work. However, in most cases it's a safe bet that if they come to you for energy work & are willing to sign your liability waiver, they understand that they will be receiving energy healing. Another, less invasive option is to ask permission from your higher self to theirs and listen/feel for an answer with your intuition.

In defense of the asking first school of thought, I'd like to impart a story that was shared by an experienced energy worker in my Reiki II class. She had been called on to do healing work on a man in a coma. She arrived and found that the family was all around the hospital bed, so she felt pressure to perform, even though she got an energetic 'no' when she tuned in and asked his higher self for permission to work on him. She placed her hands on him & his whole body jolted. Apparently his spirit had been traveling and was immediately shot back into his body when she began. She didn't do any harm, but it was still a shock to his system.

The other way of looking at this is to consider whether you'd ask before sending love. Aside from dire situations like the one mentioned in the last paragraph, energy sent with positive intent can do no harm. Our higher selves and energy fields will often deflect any energy that is not for our highest good. Some believe that whatever energy we send out will bounce back to us if it is unable to reach the object of our intention. What do you feel about this topic? As with all other things, I suggest that you follow your internal guidance in each individual situation. For this reason it is of the utmost importance to develop your intuition in order to be the best possible energy healer you can be.

Highest Good

Another common inquiry involved with energy work involves the idea of everything working for the highest good. As healers, we often feel responsible for the outcome of each session. However, the ego must not be involved in a healing. We are simply there to bring the highest vibration and best intention we can to any session. It is possible for the recipient to have blocks/barriers to receiving, or for our stated intention not to actually be for the highest good of the client. It is not for us to decide what a session or its outcome will look like. Surrender to bringing only what is for the highest good of all and let all expectation go.

Occasionally there will be a person who does not resonate with our energy. It is important to recognize that this is not personal. The top priority is to offer the best possible energy for each individual, and to understand that sometimes your energy just isn't going to mesh with theirs in a positive way. Explain this, and refer them to someone you feel they may connect with instead. You will know this is happening if you feel highly uncomfortable around them, or are feeling a strong resistance to your words and energy from them.

Attunements

An attunement is simply the act of having your vibrational levels activated and raised so that your body becomes the perfect vessel for the energy. Once you are attuned to most healing modalities, you become a conduit for healing vibration from the Universe. The energy passes through you, via the energy centers in your body- called chakras. Energy flows in through the crown of your head, travels through these chakras and flows out through your palms to whomever you are treating. The energy passing from your hands to them (or to yourself) helps to remove blockages in their system, allowing their body/mind/spirit to heal itself as intended. With Essence Healing, it is similar, but more intense. You become a physical vessel, merging with your Essence in order to send energy.

Ordinarily, a Master of a specific modality attunes students to that modality through a ceremony using symbols, visualizations and ritual. Early in my journey I came across the information that we are capable of attuning ourselves to anything- especially if we are in touch with our Essence. Our higher self is in touch with everything, everywhere and the information needed to activate you is there simply through intention and asking.

In the digital bonus material, you will find a series of MP3s in the file 'Activation Meditations.' These are intended to guide you through the process of attuning yourself to Essence healing. They walk you through everything you need to prepare for and receive your activation of Essence Healing. These were recorded during a group training class on a Saturday morning in my downtown office. The Universe saw fit to have fire engines and motorcycles going by throughout the process as part of the energy, so I've left them in. The energy of these recordings is powerful and highly effective.

Energy Detox

After an attunement, the higher vibration energy will be intertwining with your own energy, slowly speeding it up to a faster, healthier vibrational level. As it does this, you may find yourself in a cleansing process. Any toxins, emotional issues or energy blockages from past traumas may surface to be healed. This is so you can be a pure open conduit for this healing level of energy.

During this process (which usually lasts about 3 weeks) it is a good idea to take better care of yourself. Make sure you're eating well, cutting out processed foods and boosting your immune system. Vitamins such as C, Zinc and B complex are good examples of immune boosters. Drink extra water to flush your system. Cut back on or eliminate stimulants such as caffeine, nicotine and sugars. Try to find time to meditate and exercise. Most importantly, practice Essence Healing for at least 20 minutes per day on yourself. It is also a great idea to get energy treatments from others as well. These guidelines are simply to make the transition more comfortable. They are not requirements, just the best way to ease yourself in. As with anything else to improve your situation, some work is required to get the best results.

Don't be surprised if you experience temporary heightened emotions or illness. This is common and normal. Using the guidelines above will be helpful in avoiding or softening these effects. Another possibility is that you will feel much better than you have in a long time. You may see colors as brighter and more "alive." You may become more in touch with your spiritual side. You will likely experience a heightening of any psychic gifts you carry because of a deeper connection with the Universe and your own spirit.

Chapter Eight

The methods and information in the next few chapters are designed to lay the groundwork for a powerful session. They are helpful suggestions, but not required in every session. Think of them as tools that your intuition will guide you in putting to use.

Calling in Helpers

Once you and your client are grounded, you can call in whomever you would like to assist with session. It is up to you whether you want to do this silently or out loud. I usually say something like this: "I now call forth our Guides, Angels, Divine Healing Teams, Soul Families, Gaia Earth Energy, and the Source of All That Is at the highest point of light- surrounding and protecting us, raising our vibrations and the vibration of this space, bringing forth your best possible healing and any guidance you are meant to receive. Setting the intention of (insert intentions here). Setting the intention for blessings, miracles and wonderful things to occur throughout this session and beyond, and for us to be able to recognize them when they come." I will then flow into channeling if a channel comes through at this point. If not, I either begin the energy work silently or say whatever I am guided to in order to relax the receiver and encourage their total surrender. You do not have to use my script, or even call in the same beings. This is just what resonates with me.

Our divine beings are waiting for us to call them for help. We have many helpers on the other side, waiting to assist us. Unfortunately, they cannot intervene on our behalf unless asked to do so. While channeling for people, I have often brought through a message that our divine beings are our equals. We should not fear them or put them on pedestals. That when we die, we return to the form they are in now, and are their peers. It is their job, and primary purpose to assist us in living our soul's purpose here on the physical plane. The more you work with these beings, the more proof and encouragement you will encounter.

Guides are beings assigned to us, usually to help us learn things or to guide us in certain situations. Angels are protectors and bring an energy of love and security to the

122

sessions. Each angel and guide will often have its own unique purpose, specialty and energy. Divine healing teams often include our guides and angels, but also consists of beings meant to bring us healing whenever we request it. A soul family is a group of spirits that we tend to work with, both in the spirit world as well as on the physical plane. These are the characters we incarnate with again and again, playing different parts for each other in order to invoke specific experiences in our lives. Gaia is the female energy of the Earth itself. This is very healing and grounding. Invoking this energy allows a better marriage of the Divine and physical aspects of our beings. Source is the highest being you believe in: God, Allah, The Universe, call it what you will. Whomever or whatever you believe to be the source and creator of everything and everyone will certainly seal the deal for a beautiful and powerful healing. Never believe that you are unworthy of calling forth this energy, or that any of these beings are too busy for you. They are limitless beings that are part of your spiritual family. It's what they're there for.

Part of an Essence Healing session is allowing your

grounded client's energy to expand and merge with that of the divine beings you call into the session. It is likely that they will feel an expansion of their energy as you verbally guide them to do so. This merging facilitates a deeper connection and ability to receive and exchange energy with them. Most people will feel amazing upon making this connection. Guide them to let go of any boundaries or shields they've unconsciously put up so that they can fully receive what is being shared with them.

On an interesting side note, Micheal Newton, author of *Journey of Souls* and *Life Between Lives* insists that angels don't exist. I believe that when he says that, he is simply not thinking outside the box. There may not be any spirits that go around in the spirit realm with wings and halos, but that doesn't mean that spirits cannot present themselves to us that way because of our mythology and psychological familiarity with the form of an angel. Divine beings will show themselves to us in ways that comfort and reassure us. They try to make themselves familiar to us so we will be open to their guidance. Angels and or guides are essentially what we become when we return to spirit or energetic form, wings or not.

Surrender

The best method for Essence Healing is to actually do nothing. Once you've grounded, just allow the energy to exude from you. You will be surprised with how powerful and effective this can be. Surrendering to your instincts and hunches is another aspect of surrendering, and that's where the rest of these techniques come in.

Blasting Energy

Begin and end each session by blasting energy and love at the recipient. Begin with the heart, sending energy from the heart toward them; follow this with each chakra, your hand, your body, your energy field, and essence. Blast this feel-good energy at them for a few minutes, while asking the divine beings around you to do the same. Intend to bliss them out completely and totally. You will intuitively know when it is time to move on.

Pushing

While doing any kind of energy work it is possible to take things to the next level by raising the vibration of the energy you're working with. For some, the following method may take some practice, while others may take to it naturally. As with everything, I feel that intention is everything, so simply asking or intending for the vibration to be boosted will work to some extent. However, I've been shown to blast the energy in a very physical way.

Taking healing to the next level is as easy as pushing. Women who've given birth know the feeling of involuntary contractions taking over and helping move things along during labor. For me, boosting the vibration of the energy has been very similar to this phenomenon. I will suddenly feel something blooming or building within me until I get to the point where I feel the only thing to do is tighten up all of my muscles. I mean every single muscle in my body. Sure if I'm around others, I may not tighten my facial muscles- since I would look mighty strange - but otherwise everything is tensed up to the point of trembling. For me, this is not intentional; it just happens. I can control it, however. I am

126

not helpless against it. I am not having a seizure. I am taking the energy within and around me, and transforming it to a new, higher vibration.

Try this out: Intend to raise the vibration of your body and the room you are in. Ask the Universe, Divine, or your Higher Self to help if you'd like. Tense up your muscles-most especially your core muscles throughout your torso, but also your arms, legs and so on. Intend for this to raise the vibration. Hold this for as long as it feels right. It is likely you'll know when it's time to stop. When you are done, observe the pleasant sensations in your body. If you are sensitive to subtle energy, you may feel the energy moving through your body or tune into the energy in the room. Either way, things should be feeling pretty good right about now.

When I've used this technique on other intuitive or sensitive people they've described either feeling the energy getting boosted or seeing dark being overtaken by light. I've had the odd inclination to do this tensing up throughout my life. When I was young it was when I was angry or feeling powerless. Later it came up as I was hugging my significant other. (Perhaps I wanted to raise their vibration so we would resonate together on a similar frequency.) It would also show up when a conversation was becoming negative. I had no idea why I would feel energy building inside of me or why I felt the need to tighten up as many muscles as I could while still looking normal to those around me. Once I began doing energy work, it all became clear. As soon as I was attuned to Reiki and began working on people, this sensation became a regular occurrence and I just trusted what I was being shown. It felt good to eventually get confirmation from other intuitives on the power and viability of this technique.

Just because you haven't felt the urge to tense up before doesn't mean you can't use this technique. This technique is not limited to use during Essence Healing; it can also be used along with any other healing modality or when you want to boost your connection with the Divine/Universe. It can also warm you if you are cold or boost your mood when you are feeling down. Here are some things you may want to try while practicing this method:

- Envision pushing energy toward the object of your

intention, by mentally directing it, while tensing up the muscles.

- Think or say "Raise it up, raise it up, raise it up..." while pushing.

- Imagine pushing energy toward the person, place or situation you are working on with the out-breath, and refilling your stores of energy by pulling from the earth and the Divine/universe with the in-breath. This focus is not necessary with every breath, just check in every so often to see that this is occurring.

- Use your breath to direct the energy focus.

- Try pushing all of the air out of your lungs for a few breaths in a row, using the muscles in your chest and abdomen to squeeze the lungs until they empty. Slowly fill them back up, and repeat for as long as it feels right.

- Use the muscles in the center of your diaphragm to squeeze air and energy up your windpipe. This feels similar to the giddiness or excitement one might feel at the top of a roller coaster, and is different from the above practice of pushing all of the air out of the lungs. You should feel this more in the center of your chest and throat, rather than your lungs.

- If your muscles begin to cramp up or spasm, take a break from this method. Keep practicing in shorter bursts until you build up stamina. You may also want to look into getting the potassium and other electrolytes in your body balanced.
- Use this technique if you feel that you are in, or are about to enter, a very low vibration situation or area.
- Use this when tapping into others in order to boost your intuition.
- Open an energy circle/meditation group with this method.
- Blast any healing modality to the highest possible level by using this technique.
- Protect yourself or others from negative/low vibration energy.

Note:

Do not hold your breath or strain the muscles in your head, as this could cause physical damage. It is normal for your heart to beat more rapidly during and after these boosting methods. They can be similar to doing a cardio workout. Check with your doctor to make sure you are healthy enough to do cardio before utilizing these techniques.

Movement

In the course of doing healing work, many people find that they feel guided to move a certain way or make specific hand motions. Sometimes these even begin to happen spontaneously. Another phenomenon is being magnetically pulled to certain areas of the recipient's body or energy field. This is your body's own intuition at work, showing you how to be the best possible conduit for healing. The more you move, the more energy can move through you. This is true both during sessions, as well as making sure you move your body for health and energy purposes at other times.

In rare cases, this can also begin happening to the recipient of energy work. I've seen people twitching, pulsating, shaking, tensing up, flopping one or multiple limbs and so on. This is not cause for concern. This actually shows that they are energetically open and will likely receive a more powerful healing for this reason. Just reassure them that what they are doing is normal and that they are just being shown what area is being worked on. Coughs, sneezes and digestive sounds are also very good signs of release. I do find that Reiki tends to produce more physical movement than Essence Healing, however. The grounding aspect of Essence Healing is more calming and tends to heal people from within, rather than forcing energy through the meridians, so less movement is needed to undo blockages with this modality.

I highly recommend that all parties involved in any session just go with the flow to the best of their ability, and of course, following legal boundaries regarding touch. Everything experienced while in energy is a valuable gift. Don't discount your body's natural knowing and opening.

Hand of God

At times, when I'm doing a session, I will ask Source/God/The Universe to take over the session and work on a particular issue or area. Once again, this is just a matter of asking and intending. Then you just stand back and continue running energy while you witness a larger force do the healing work for you. It's pretty fun to observe, especially once you've learned how to tune into what's going on on an energetic level.

Another extraordinary thing you can request for your client is a "God Flush." This is an energetic and divine flush of all systems on all levels of the person's being: the energetic systems of the meridians and chakras, the physical systems of the body and so on. Watch what happens when you request this and surrender the session to a higher energy.

In Chapter Nine I describe the chakras at length. Meridians are energy channels that run throughout the body connecting one area to another energetically. These are the energy channels that therapies such as acupuncture and Shiatsu focus on most. The meridian system is quite complex and beyond my scope of specialty. You may Google "energy meridians" to get more information and visuals. I recommend trusting that your intention is enough to activate the flushing of these systems without having to learn and memorize them. The same goes for the body and its systems.

Soul Fragments

Over the course of this lifetime as well as other lifetimes, we encounter various traumas- both large and small. At these moments, it is believed that our spirits leave our bodies. A piece of our Essence gets left at the place of this trauma or becomes imbedded in someone else involved in the trauma. In order to make your Essence whole again, you can call these soul fragments back to you. Once again, this is accomplished simply by using your intention. You get into a relaxed and open state, and then command that all of your soul fragments be returned to you- cleansed and purified. There is an MP3 guided meditation in the bonus digital material that will walk you through this process. This can be done during a session for your client as well.

Wandering Mind

While performing energy work, you are deeply tuned in to whomever you are working on. We are all trained to attempt to quiet our minds while doing energy work, but I would like to offer an alternate point of view.

When I first began doing Reiki, I noticed that I was feeling what was going on inside my clients' energy fields and bodies. I could feel, in my own body, where they had pain and blockages- as though my body suddenly had those issues. I used this to my advantage while working on them- as I knew exactly where I needed to focus the energy and for how long. Once I became accustomed to working with energy, I noticed that my mind would begin wandering during sessions. At first I tried to bring my focus back to the client & would gently chastise myself for thinking about my own life. Then it finally hit me. If I could physically become my clients while I worked on them, what if I was also mentally becoming them?

I began paying attention to my thoughts whenever I did energy work and mentioning them to my clients. If I thought about a break up I once had, it was likely they were dealing with a breakup. If a song or a scene from a movie popped into my head it had something to do with their life. I even found that if I thought about me, it was about them- but if I thought about a situation that a friend or family member had going on, it was a friend or family member of theirs that they were concerned about. I was astounded to have these thoughts confirmed as intuitive messages again and again.

You are just as capable of picking up on this as I am. Here's how it works: Every single thing in the universe has its own unique vibrational frequency. A toothache, a heart attack, a breakup each has its own vibration. We all walk around with the frequencies of what we are focused on or experiencing within our energy fields. Someone who is open/sensitive can easily pick up on these vibrations within the energy fields close to them, or in those they are tuned into (thinking about.) Energy work makes us all sensitive and open. Doing energy healing work is a great way to develop intuition.

As I mentioned before, you may think you are not intuitive because you've been expecting it to show up in a specific way. Clairvoyance is the most recognized psychic ability in our culture, but it is also one of the most rare. If you are expecting to see visions, you could be missing out on information coming in through another one of your other senses.

Our intuition works much like our brain works, since it

is our brain translating the frequency of each thing into something we can understand. If you are highly visual you may have visions or see colors and lights others can't see. However, if you tend to be more auditory or physically aware, or if you think in words rather than images, it will be extremely difficult and unlikely for you to have visions.

Clairvoyance is intuition that is sight based, clairaudience is based on hearing, clairsentience is a sudden understanding of words or ideas within your mind, there are even rare gifts of clairolfactance (smell) and clairgustance (taste.) The most common, but least recognized psychic ability is physical, and people with this ability are referred to as Empaths.

Empaths have the ability to feel what is going on around them energetically. First, I want to explain that there is a difference between being an Empath and having empathy. Let's use the toothache example again: a guy comes into the room you're in right now and he has a toothache. If you were an Empath, you will usually experience a toothache without consciously knowing that the man has a toothache. An empathetic person, however, would be able to create the sensation of a toothache in themselves, but only once they are told about the toothache. The Empath has picked up on the frequency of the toothache and their brain translated it into a physical sensation to show them what's going on nearby. The empathetic person doesn't replicate the sensation of a toothache until made aware of it on a conscious level, if at all.

Something to keep in mind if you're an Empath- you are not actually taking on other peoples stuff. Your physical sensations are exactly the same as a clairvoyant vision- except physical rather than visual- it is simply your brain translating vibrational information into a language you can understand. The trouble comes when we don't realize we're being shown someone else's issues and believe they belong to us. As I said before, a clairvoyant person doesn't spend the day seeing someone's tooth once they've recognized it as relating to someone else. An Empath need not feel others pain once they pinpoint it as belonging to someone else. Take it as information, disconnect from it and move on. Grounding or intentionally pulling your energy field in closer to your body will also help protect you from carrying around the things you pick up on from others.

Regardless of how your intuition works, I encourage you to pay attention to all of your senses, including your thoughts, as you do energy work. Take in everything that happens: what do you hear, smell, taste, see, think about and feel? Go over these experiences with your client after the session and see what resonates with them. The more you do this, the more you will learn to trust and expand your intuition.

Chapter Nine

Chakras

Below is a diagram of the seven primary chakras. There are several other chakras in our energy bodies, but these are the seven most recognized and influential. There are several parts of Essence Healing sessions that involve the chakras, so this chapter will help familiarize you with what they do and what they mean, as well as going into more detailed instructions on integrating them into treatments.

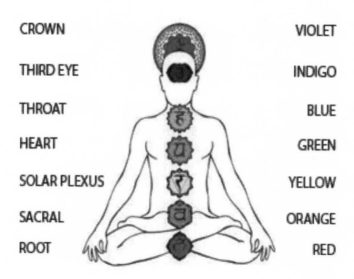

CROWN   VIOLET

THIRD EYE   INDIGO

THROAT   BLUE

HEART   GREEN

SOLAR PLEXUS   YELLOW

SACRAL   ORANGE

ROOT   RED

Chakras are energy centers through which our life-force energy flows. Each chakra represents a different aspect of life. This is a brief overview of the individual chakras, as well as the statements that represent them. You will find a more detailed guide to chakra blockages and their meanings at the end of this chapter.

- The crown is the highest Chakra and it represents our ability to be fully connected spiritually. It also is related to inner and outer beauty, our energetic openness, faith, and bliss. "I understand."

- The third eye concerns our ability to focus on and see the big picture. Intuition, imagination, wisdom, the ability to think and make decisions are all major aspects of this energy center. "I see."

- The throat chakra is related to our ability to communicate. Speaking your heart, self-expression of feelings, the truth are what this chakra is all about. "I speak."

- The heart chakra focuses on our ability to love and intimately connect with others. Love, generosity, joy, and inner peace are represented here. "I love."

- The solar plexus chakra is connected with our ability to be confident and in control of our lives. This chakra is primarily concerned with self-worth, self-confidence, and self-esteem. The ego has been known to be centered here. "I think."

- The sacral chakra pertains to our connection and ability to accept others and new experiences as well as our ability to create. Our Sense of abundance, well-being, romantic relationships, creativity, pleasure, and sexuality all live here. "I feel."

- The root chakra represents our foundation and sense of being grounded. Survival issues such as financial independence, money, and food as well as our ability to feel secure in our relationships, work and overall safety are centered here. "I am."

Following are a few techniques you can use during healing work related to the chakras.

Blasting Energy from the Chakras

Begin with your heart Chakra. It may help to simply envision your heart as a green ball of light. Open your heart. Mentally let go of any barriers or shields you've subconsciously placed here, and start sending out love energy. Pay attention to how this feels, so you are familiar with the sensation of sending from a chakra. You may wish to combine this technique with one of the pushing or breathing techniques.

Continue this process with each of the other chakras in the order that is most comfortable for you, while continuing to send from the chakras you've already activated. If you like specific guidelines, I'd suggest this order: Heart, Solar, Sacral, Root, Throat, Third Eye, Crown. But seriously, do your own thing! Once you have this technique down, you will no longer need to activate them separately; you will just intend for your chakras to be blasting energy and they will be.

Flossing Chakras

This technique is one of those that just happened because I trusted my body to show me what to work on. One day I noticed I was standing with my hands spread out above my client's body and pushing energy through the chakras, back and forth between my palms. I began to feel guided to do this in nearly every session soon after. At first I had no idea what it accomplished, but eventually I began to understand that it worked to align, balance, connect and heal the chakras- as well as clear an energetic channel for Kundalini energy to pass through.

I hold my hands about 4-6 inches above the body with one hand slightly above the top of the head (crown chakra) and one just below the tailbone (root chakra.) I then begin to envision my hands lower, even though I keep them up at the same height above the body. I picture sending energy from palm to palm through each of the 7 primary chakras and intend that they be connected, aligned, cleansed, healed, opened, and activated. I often use pushing and rock my body back and forth while doing this. You will naturally know when to stop, but I find it's usually only necessary to floss for a few minutes for most people.

Another option is to envision their chakras rising up out of the body to meet your hand alignment. This is just as viable as picturing your hands lowering. I also find this imagery helpful when I am drawn to work on a specific chakra. I will envision it rising up above the person's body, do whatever work needs to be done to it, then picture it glowing and lowering back into place.

Blessing Chakras

Toward the end of a session, I will often use a Tibetan singing bowl over each chakra and envision its corresponding color filling the chakra as well as the areas of the body that are related to that chakra. A singing bowl amplifies the energy, but it is not necessary. There are tones that specifically resonate with each chakra, so if you love music you may want to look into tonal therapy and sound healing. However, this technique works beautifully to harmonize the chakras with or without sound. Placing crystals that resonate with the various chakras can also

146

amplify energy. The following diagram shows the way I envision the colors as I intentionally bless each chakra, beginning at the root and moving up each chakra systematically. In my mind, as I stand above each chakra, I silently say "(appropriate color) blessing for this chakra and all that it is related to" while imagining the color filling that entire area. Red at the root, orange for sacral, yellow in the solar plexus, green for the heart, blue at the throat, indigo for the third eye and violet at the crown.

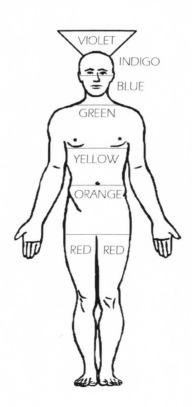

Chakra Readings

I will often tune in to people's chakras in order to discover more about their struggles in life. Nearly all physical issues one have an emotional basis and these emotions show in the chakras first. The premise I go by as far as connecting physical maladies to emotional energy blocks comes from such books as *You Can Heal Your Life* by Louise Hay and *Feelings Buried Alive Never Die* by Karol K. Truman.

The concept is that we have an experience (betrayal for example), and a resulting emotion (hurt/sadness/heartbreak). If we accept and allow that emotion to fully express itself, it moves on through as it should. However, most of us were taught not to express or even feel our emotions. If the emotion comes up and we ignore it, attempt to drown or subdue it, it sticks with us, waiting to get noticed. Depending on what this emotion is related to (i.e. in this example-romantic connectedness/trust), it gets stored in different parts of the energy field (heart chakra). When enough blockage has occurred in one area, it begins to manifest physical symptoms in the body and mind in a corresponding area (ie. heart, lungs, back) as a way of getting your attention. Essentially, in simpler terms, your heart was broken and now it's physically breaking from the weight of that loss staying with you.

Of course, family history can affect health conditions; sometimes these patterns of emotional backup are also passed down a family line in the same way, as well as nutritional choices, beliefs and lifestyle habits. These all play a part in creating our level of health, but when you boil it all back down, it can be brought back to our emotional base and whether we are free to feel or not. As this is the biggest thing that is passed down again and again through family lines it affects all other aspects of our lives. For instance, if one felt whole and complete, would they need to take part in addiction, overeating, shopping, gambling, drinking... in order to feel better?

There is so much you can learn about someone from tuning into the chakras. Pay attention to how you feel in each of your energy centers when you interact with someone. This will often show you where they are blocked or imbalanced. You can then use this information combined with the guidance below to read the chakras. I have used this technique at many events to recruit new clients. I tune into them, find the 3 most uncomfortable chakras and discuss the points below. I then suggest energy healing and intuitive coaching as a possible path to healing these issues. People are often amazed by what I know about them just by feeling their chakra energy. Oh and just a heads-up, you will likely find that the throat and solar plexus chakras are the most commonly "off" in our culture, due to our social conditioning.

The root chakra (at the base of your tailbone) relates to your sense of security and stability. Not feeling safe, secure, supported in any aspect of your life or money fears and traumas can all block or imbalance this Chakra.

Body parts connected to the root energy center are:
- feet
- legs
- knees
- hips

- tailbone
- genitals
- reproductive glands (male)
- bladder

The sacral chakra (lower abdomen) pertains to your creativity. It is the womb center- so anything having to do with "creation" is centered here. Creative and/or sexual expression and relationships live here. If any of these have been squelched or disappointing, that's when a blockage or imbalance occurs.

Body parts & issues related to the sacral energy center:
- hormonal imbalances
- reproductive and sexual organs
- lower digestive system
- lower back/sacrum/hips
- appendix

The solar plexus (stomach level) houses your sense of who you believe you are and how you think things work. It is your center of empowerment and pride. This chakra pertains to wanting to control things to go the way you want/expect them to, or believe they should be, rather than trusting that things are exactly as they should be, that the universe wants more for you than you could ever want for yourself. There is also an element that affects this chakra related to worrying about the past or the future, rather than being fully in the moment. Another aspect of this is your sense of self, and beliefs about how life works. So issues can arise if your beliefs are challenged.

Body parts/issues associated with the solar plexus energy center:

- upper digestive system
- ulcers
- stomach
- anxiety
- gall bladder
- spleen
- kidneys
- liver
- middle back

The heart chakra relates to the level of intimacy you can allow in your life and your connection with others. Trust issues often lead to blocked heart chakras. If there is a protective wall around your heart nothing good can get in or out. Envision a door in front of your heart, open it with your mind and ask the universe to fill it with all that is meant for you to receive, and just feel the flow for a few minutes.

Body parts/issues related to the heart energy center:

- heart
- lungs
- breasts
- circulation
- arms
- hands
- upper back
- depression

The throat is about needing to speak your truth. Most of us have this issue because we're "encouraged" to bottle it up early on, and never learn the valuable tool of communicating in a gentle way that gets your needs met but doesn't blame the other person for not automatically knowing.

The throat chakra being off track can effect:
- neck
- throat
- thyroid
- sinuses
- jaw
- teeth
- shoulders
- ears
- depression

The third eye chakra (mid forehead)- surrounds our intuition/trusting inner wisdom and your openness to receiving spiritual energy/ wisdom. If you have any fear surrounding psychic abilities or mistrusting your natural intuition, the third eye tends to get backed up- causing eye/vision issues, headaches and living in your head a lot.

154

Body parts associated with the third eye energy center:

- eyes
- pituitary & pineal glands
- lower portion of brain
- upper sinuses

As for the crown (just above the top of the head), we are in a time of huge transition (The Shift). The earth's vibration is rising exponentially right now and for many of us who are not used to such an intensely high vibration are experiencing much discomfort. So many people feel that 'something is coming' or building and this can bring great fear and a tendency to close up even further to protect ourselves- which will only make things harder. This time is about going with the flow, rather than swimming upstream. It has become a time for sudden spiritual awakening and feeling tested and tortured until that part of you is opened up. If you notice a lot of headaches, this is often related to the amount of universal love energy trying to get in, as opposed to the width of your channel for receiving. Many people, women especially, have very tiny receiving channels because we've learned only to give. Now is the time to receive. If the crown is blocked we tend to get mired in fear and ego, forgetting who and what we truly are- we also may begin to have brain issues or mental illness.

Here's an exercise you can recommend for someone with an issue at the crown. When a headache comes, envision the top of your skull opening upward and outward like a funnel. Allow yourself to receive all that exists in the universe that is meant for you- keep opening there and in your heart.

Any and all of these blockages can be from (and usually are) past and present times that emotions related to these chakras have been ignored or suppressed in some way. Sitting quietly just feeling the areas in your body that feel heavy to you can go a long way toward healing them, especially when fully grounded in your body. All they want is a little recognition.

Chapter Ten

Kundalini

Kundalini is the Eastern name for dormant energy within us that can be activated in order to bring about spiritual awakening. This can be initiated by various means: meditation, energy work, an attunement called Shaktipat given by a guru, intention or can sometimes be set off by a traumatic experience. Kundalini can also sometimes activate spontaneously for no apparent reason. I would take this to mean that your soul chose this time for you to awaken. Traditionally, this energy is visualized as a serpent made of pure energy that lives at the base of our spine or within the root chakra. Keep in mind that serpents do not have the same negative connotation in other cultures as it does in ours. This energy serpent remains in hibernation until an awakening is triggered, then it begins to coil upward through the chakras, activating each one as it goes. This is meant to allow energy to flow freely through your entire system, and is often accompanied by a shifting in consciousness.

While this process unfolds over varying periods of time distinctive to each person, it can have myriad effects- both positive and negative. When the awakening is intended and fully allowed, it is called a Kundalini Awakening. However, if the awakening is thrust upon you or you resist the effects, it can become what is often referred to as Kundalini Syndrome. I have most commonly seen the syndrome reaction in people who've had a strict Christian upbringing that has trained them that intuition and related abilities and experiences are evil. This often causes them to misinterpret their experiences, as well as creating the expectation of evil to appear - which then invokes the experience of evil within their minds. Any level of mental imbalance will intensify this dynamic, so it is important for anyone with these qualities to seek the consul of a mental health professional who is open minded to metaphysical or spiritual matters to guide them in ways that acknowledge the spiritual journey while caring for the mental state as the awakening occurs.

There is also a premise that many perceived mental illnesses are actually caused by Kundalini Awakenings/Syndrome or by spiritual/energetic attachments (commonly referred to as possession, but is not nearly as horrible as Hollywood portrays it to be.) This is not always the case, but it is generally a good idea to clear their energy fields of attachments, just in case. See 'Releasing Entities' in Chapter Six for more information.

Kundalini Awakening/Syndrome

The following are all possible signs or symptoms of Kundalini Awakening/Syndrome:

- Spontaneous sexual sensation or arousal
- Feeling energy or sensation moving upward through the feet and legs up into the body
- Twitching, trembling, shaking or vibrating of the body or parts of the body
- The urge to breathe in certain patterns for no apparent reason
- The urge to move the body in certain ways for no apparent reason
- Tingling, heat or cold in the palms of the hands
- Tingling, heat or cold sensations moving through the

body, especially up the spine or just under the skin

- Feeling as though you are shrinking or expanding in comparison to the energy around you
- Hearing internal sounds or voices with no explicable external source
- Seeing colors, lights or bright flashes like stars with no explicable external source
- Being in a dark room with the eyes closed, yet feeling that the room is brightly lit
- Observing yourself as though from outside the self
- Experiencing spontaneous bliss, peace, love, ecstasy, joy, or connection with everything
- Experiencing spontaneous hatred, anger, fear, confusion and loneliness/separation
- Having headaches more frequently than usual
- Feeling pressure on top of the head or in the center of the forehead
- Seeing Orbs, lights and shadows with no logical explanation
- Knowing things before they happen
- Feeling the urge to put your hands on someone for

healing purposes

• Experiencing a second puberty, in which you become very sexual and hormonal

As you can imagine, it can be quite frightening to experience some of these without knowing their cause. Some of these may also resemble physical or mental illness. This is often because the energy is clearing things from our system that no longer need to be there. Plus our culture has a tendency to fear what it does not understand; so spiritual awakening and intuition can often be misinterpreted. That's when it becomes a syndrome rather than an awakening. Fear and resistance are what makes the difference.

The best way to traverse this transition is to first recognize what is occurring. Pay attention to your experiences and compare them with this list. Do your best to allow this unfolding to occur in the most peaceful way possible. Surrender as best you can. If you experience things you perceive as negative, try to acknowledge that it is likely you are purging something that doesn't serve you. You may also want to seek out a medical professional who understands and respects the spiritual journey. You can also reach out to a local energy worker or intuitive life coach in your community who can help guide you, if you are not necessarily concerned about your physical or mental well-being, but would like guidance.

Many spiritual seekers actually desire this awakening. After all, it activates the intuition, healing abilities and allows for energy to flow through our bodies and energy centers keeping us balanced and healthy in many ways. As long as you know what you are getting yourself into, this can be an enjoyable part of your journey.

Performing a Kundalini Awakening

During an Essence Healing session you may intend for your client to receive a Kundalini Awakening for their highest good, while envisioning energy coiling in a spiral up through their chakras. You may experience a knowing that certain chakras are closed to this energy. The intention is that the Kundalini energy continue working on those chakras, in the gentlest possible way, until they open and allow the energy to flow through. It is highly recommended

162

that your own Kundalini be activated before you perform this service on others. You can do this through intention, visualization and meditation. As I've mentioned, people can experience symptoms of awakening that can range from ecstatic to hellish. This is why you want to intend the awakening occur for their highest good.

Chapter Eleven

Healing with Essence

These are the basic steps to begin Essence Healing. Prepare to feel amazing!

- Begin by grounding your Essence into your body and raising your vibration.
- Intend or verbally guide the recipient to bring their Essence in and raise their vibration to match it.
- Surrender. Begin allowing energy to just exude from you naturally.
- Bring your awareness to your heart chakra and allow energy to flow from this area. Think, "I love you. I love you soooo freaking much! I am bursting with love for you..." and allow these feelings to flow from your heart chakra in the form of energy toward the subject of your healing.
- Follow the last step with each of the other chakras and then from all of them at once.
- Send energy from your skin.

- Allow energy to flow from every part of your body.

- Beam energy from every cell, molecule, and atom of your being. There are more cells in our bodies than stars in the solar system. Envision sending energy from every one of them.

- Let your energy field send healing energy and love.

- Intend for your entire being to send the most powerful energy it can muster, sourced by your oneness with your Essence.

- Occasionally, pull in from the Earth and the Divine to refill your Essence.

- Observe/feel your energy entering and merging with the recipient's energy field.

- Check in to make sure you are both remaining grounded.

- Continue sending from everywhere you've got- go ahead, let it bliss you out. The better you feel, the better they feel.

Note:

The more you practice this process, the faster and more

effortless this will become. You will be able to just intend to send from everywhere and have it happen instantaneously. You will likely feel your individual cells vibrating, as you become more and more sensitive to subtle energy activity (as opposed to the non-subtlety of our average physical existence). Once you get the hang of it, you'll be executing this modality while walking down the street.

In order to experience the difference between healing while grounded and ungrounded, I suggest trying it both ways. Intend for your Essence to temporarily vacate your body and send healing energy. Have the recipient try this as well. It is likely you will be able to feel a distinct difference when everyone is grounded vs. ungrounded. Make sure you reground when you're finished trying this out.

Steps for Professional Essence Healing Sessions

The following is a list of steps I use when performing an Essence Healing session on a client. It is not required that you follow these exact steps in order. You may even skip certain steps. The only elements that are required are the techniques marked with an asterisk*. Allow yourself to be guided by your intuition as you perform Essence Healing.

- Consult with your client about what they would like the session to focus on. This could be anything. They may desire pain relief, healing of a physical issue, mental or emotional balancing, or setting the intention for a situation in their life to be healed.

- Get clear about their expectations and describe what they might experience/expect throughout the session. This can range from seeing colors and lights to feeling energy move through them. They may also simply feel deeply relaxed, or have various memories and emotions come through.

- Let them know that they should allow whatever comes through- thoughts, memories, movements, emotions, etc. What they experience shows them what is being worked on.

- *Ground yourself by mentally pulling your Essence into your body, then intending that your body and brain be raised to its vibration. (See 'Grounding' in Chapter

One for more detailed instructions.) You may want to have your client breathe slow deep breaths into the bottom of their lungs as you mentally ground yourself.

- Allow healing energy to begin to flow and place your hands on the client's shoulders.

- *Surrender and exude energy.

- Begin to bring yourself and your client into the Theta brainwave state. Walk your client through a progressive relaxation exercise of your choosing. You will be tuned into them, so you will know when they've become relaxed by feeling how tense/relaxed you are.

- Help your client tune in to any discomfort and fully allow/appreciate it.

- Help them to release any shields, boundaries, and walls.

- *Guide your client in calling in their Essence, integrating it, and raising their vibration. Let them know this is how they were meant to feel. This is their true self.

- Guide them in expanding their energy outward to merge with divine beings, while remaining grounded. Call in guides, angels, divine healing teams, soul families, Source, etc.

- Set intentions for the session.

- Channel if desired/able.

- *Begin the process of Essence Healing: Send from your chakras (heart first), then hands, physical body, cells, molecules, atoms, energy field, Essence. Refill from earth & divine as needed. You may do only this for the remainder of the session or use any/all of the following techniques along with Essence.

- Allow your mind to wander as you beam energy at your client. Whatever you are thinking about or feeling will likely have something to do with them. Your energy is linked with theirs and you're picking up on their frequency- like picking up a radio signal.

- Push energy by using muscle tension & breath in order to intensify the healing and direct the flow of energy.

- *Allow your body to move as it feels guided to do. You

170

may notice your body naturally swaying or undulating with the flow of energy, or tensing up on its own to push energy. Some people experience an inner knowing of ways to move their arms or hands in order to heal something. Let it happen!!! Your body knows how to best send energy.

- Play with placing your hands on the recipient as well as not touching them. I found that I was able to feel energy more when I wasn't touching the person, when I first began energy healing. Over time I began to be able to feel it either way. Trust your intuition on what to do in each area, and with each person.

- Floss out the chakras by placing your hands above the recipient's body- with one hand above the root chakra and one above the crown. Intend for energy to flow from your hands, energetically "flossing" the chakras. Intending that they become aligned, healed, cleared, and activated.

- Hold your hands above the heart and solar plexus chakras, palms up, as though you are holding a small baby there. Call their essence into your hands, then rock & cradle it. Pour all of your love into it. Ask your divine helpers to do the same. When you feel this step is complete, pour the Essence back into the body and envision it filling them back up with golden light and glowing outward.

- Call in Source to work on an area or issue.

- Ask for them to receive a God Flush of all of their systems.

- Clear off any dark/negative/low vibration energy they have within or around them. Tune into whatever you observe about them that doesn't serve them and begin energetically brushing it off, pulling it out, beating on it, scooping it out, lifting it off, beaming energy at it, tossing it into a pit and blowing it up or sending it into the light- whatever feels right to you at the moment. Make sure to refill the areas you remove things from by filling them with light, blasting Essence at them. Another option here is to ask that it be raised in vibration, therefore transitioned from a negative to a positive.

- Scan for entities and attachments and release them into

the light. Replace with light.

- Bless each individual chakra by standing over it and envisioning its proper color, filling that chakra and the sector of the body associated with it. You may also use crystals, singing bowls, or vocal toning to open each chakra as you are above it.

- Send one last blast of Essence and love at them from your entire being. Ask your divine helpers to do the same.

- Stand at the foot of the table. Envision your chakras sending out connectors to theirs. Root to root, sacral to sacral and so on. See a swirl of light flow from you up through their chakras, spiraling up from their root to their crown and intend that they receive a Kundalini awakening for their highest and best good. (You must have activated Kundalini within yourself first.)

- *Close the ceremony with whatever you see fit: sound healing, vocal toning, ohms, setting more intentions, a short prayer, and so on. Get creative! Make sure you ground yourself and your client one last time, mentally, as you close out your session.

- You may also want to intend that any psychic ties (energetic bonds that keep a person linked with others, often in negative ways), karmic bonds (energetic links lasting throughout various lifetimes, keeping them stuck in old patterns) and soul contracts (contracts they've made with others and themselves on the spirit plane that may be keeping them from moving on in this lifetime) that no longer serve them be severed, healed, and released. (It is highly recommended that you have done this practice on yourself first.)

- Discuss whatever you pick up on about them during the session and ask about their experience. Explain anything you can about what they describe from their perspective.

- Recommend that they practice the grounding technique every chance they get- most especially when they feel tense or "off." Make any recommendations of other practices or books you feel would help them on their path.

Self-Healing

To use Essence Healing on yourself, simply ground and allow the energy to move through and around you. You may use any of the above techniques to amplify the session. I recommend self-healing daily, especially if you feel as though you are coming down with something. I've gone 5 years without getting sick. Every time I feel something coming on I immediately perform some energy work on myself.

I suggest practicing all of the above techniques in order to get familiar with them, but to allow sessions to guide themselves. I teach these myriad methods so that you have endless options in each individual session. Once you are familiar with all of the different techniques you can just be playful and let your instincts guide you.

Essence Healing in Everyday Life

Once you've gotten the techniques of grounding and raising your vibration down, the sky is the limit on how you can put them to use. Much of this book is focused on how to use it in healing sessions, but there is so much more you can do with it. I can't recommend strongly enough practicing entering the Essence state as often as possible and applying it to your daily activities and interactions. You can use it to heal yourself, set intentions for manifesting your desires, send positive or healing energy to people, places, situations, animals, plants and the planet. You could send transformational intentions to events in the past or the future. This may also be used to improve any relationship in your life, and it can absolutely improve intimacy and your sex life.

It is also important to recognize that you don't have to open a healing practice in order to heal yourself and others. This modality can have an effect on everyone you interact with, even if you work at a bank, school, office, farm or law firm. When you apply Essence to your life, you are affecting change regardless of what you do for work.

To use Essence Healing for any of the above purposes, simply follow the procedure described in the section labeled Grounding in Chapter One. Once you've achieved a fully grounded and higher vibrational state, sit quietly and observe the energy moving through you in combination with the following methods for each intention.

- **Self-healing**: Intend for your Essence and the energy to heal you for your highest good. Hold for as long as you'd like. You'll know when you're done. You can also set the intention to continue this healing all night as you sleep peacefully and deeply.

- **Manifesting**: Focus on a mantra or affirmation that states your desire as though it has already come true. For example: I am in perfect health, I make $100,000 per year or more, I have a passionate love life, etc. Intend for your vibration to be raised to match those desires being manifested. Feel into that vibration and/or the emotions you'd feel if you had those things for at least 90 seconds. Blast Essence energy at the intentions as well. Being in the Theta brainwave state makes this even more powerful.

- **Sending energy to people places, situations and so on**: Picture the person, place or thing you'd like to improve. Envision them/it with your ideal outcome for at least 90 seconds. Send Essence energy as guided. Fair warning, you cannot affect the free will of others. It's more helpful to see yourself at peace no matter what than to try to make someone else change to suit your needs. Also, if it isn't possible for the change you are envisioning to spontaneously occur, you may have an epiphany regarding action you can take to effect the desired change while you are meditating on it or shortly after.

- **Healing the Past/Future**: Envision the event (whether past or future) being surrounded by light or high vibration energy. Send Essence energy from your entire being to this event. Observe/allow healing to occur for the past events & the people involved. Intend for future events to be divinely guided for the highest good and place an energy bubble around them that only allows energy that resonates at the frequency of love or higher in.

- **Improving Relationships**: Picture you and the person whose relationship you wish to affect, together, with high vibration energy moving through and around you both, severing any negative ties & building new healthy connections between you- feeling the way you would like to feel with this person and acknowledging of any

178

thoughts/feelings you've been having that are painful-intending they be transmuted (changed) for the highest good of you both. Blast Essence energy toward both of you & your bond. Another clever trick is to mentally send your higher self on a mission to speak to their higher self on the spirit plane in order to work out any differences or misunderstandings between you. This often clears issues effortlessly on the physical plane.

- **Intimacy and Sexual Enhancement**: Teach your partner this grounding process and take time for both of you to ground & resonate at a higher frequency at the beginning of any sexual encounter or intimate activity. Send each other Essence energy; let it be the atmosphere you interact within. Even arguments and serious discussions can be drastically improved if both of you take the time to get into this state of wholeness. Throughout any encounter, make sure to continue reminding yourself to remain in that state and envisioning your partner there as well. Even if your partner is unable/unwilling to participate, you can still ground yourself. Trust your intuition as to whether you envision them grounded as well.

Chapter Twelve

Manifesting Your Desires

In the mid eighties, Esther Hicks began channeling a group of divine beings who identified themselves as Abraham. The information she channeled was the basis for the entire Law of Attraction movement. The premise is that you can create, attract and manifest everything you want by concentrating on it and resonating with it. Of course, there are various other tricks and stipulations to applying this principle, but that's the general idea.

The most common method you will see suggested to manifest things is this: Spend 90 seconds or more imagining that you have what you want. Feel it, taste it, smell it, see it. Allow every sense to experience having your desire fulfilled. Combining this with grounding makes it even more powerful. Doing this in Theta super boosts it. All of this is meant to help you vibrationally resonate in harmony with the desire itself, plus implants it into your subconscious, therefore drawing it to you.

It is my assertion, however, that your ability to manifest is only as powerful as your belief in that ability. In my experience, you can spend all the time and energy in the world wishing for something, but if part of you chimes in and says "That's not possible." or "You're not worthy of that," it's just not going to happen. Your intention, regarding manifesting, is only as powerful as the percentage of your brain that believes. It is also very important that you resonate at the vibrational frequency of your desires, and you can't do that if you doubt them.

The year that I spent learning about the Theta brainwave state was one of the most revolutionary years of my life. It was as though I was receiving a Universal degree in meditation and hypnosis. At the end of that year, I came across a piece of information that made everything I had been learning fall right into place. It turns out that we are being programmed with our parents' energy and beliefs from conception on. We spend most of our lives, from the time we begin developing a brain until we're about 6 or 7 years old, in the Theta state. This is one of the most programmable states we can be in- so everything we see, hear, think, feel, perceive and get told is programmed into us as the truth. Even if we become more enlightened on a conscious level as we mature, our subconscious mind is still running all of those old beliefs and programs- most of which are untrue and unhealthy.

The culmination of that year's findings led me to develop my hypnosis program, which I called Metamorphosis. I would like to share with you the steps to completely reprogram your brain and revolutionize your life. I have an entire program already set up, which I usually charge hundreds of dollars for, and you're going to learn an even more effective version right here in this book.

If the following protocol seems overwhelming, I do have a few prerecorded versions with some of the most popular programs already included that you can purchase to try out for a minimal donation. It's likely that once you see what begins to change in your life, you will want to continue this process with programs specific to you. There is also a recording in the bonus digital material called Resonance Programs, which will give you a taste of resonating with your desires as well as how these hypnosis programs work. Check out the mp3 recording by listening once every night as you sleep for a month or so, and see how you feel. It's a raw recording I did for myself, but others ended up enjoying.

To give you an idea of the benefits, this is the write up I use to present the Metamorphosis program to people at events:

What is holding you back? You have the best of intentions, yet you don't reach your goals and potential. Your mind is the only thing standing between you and ALL of your dreams.

We all know that children learn rapidly. One reason for this is that young children spend most of their time in the Theta brainwave state, which is the state of imagination and daydreaming. This is a highly open and receptive state in which the mind becomes highly impressionable. The information taken in during this state shapes ones inner truth. The downside of being in this state is that we become programmed by everything we encounter, whether positive or negative. This creates a dynamic in which nearly every idea we encounter before the age of seven become our default beliefs. What did your parents, society, and church teach you in that time? What did you decide was true and false about yourself and the world? What was the attitude toward you? How were you treated? How were others treated in front of you? What did your family believe was good, bad, possible and impossible?

It was unavoidable to receive this early programming. This has affected your life and beliefs ever since. Even if you've achieved a mental state of enlightenment within your conscious mind, these scripts still govern your ever-present subconscious mind. The subconscious mind controls your reactions to everything you encounter. This is why you cannot fully find peace within yourself, and why you haven't created the life of your dreams on the outside. Your subconscious mind is running programs that are at odds with your conscious intentions. This affects all aspects of your life.

The Metamorphosis is a simple technique, where you get to choose what to believe and what you want your life to look like and have it programmed in while you sleep. The trick is getting you back into the brainwave state that opens your subconscious as much as possible, while plugging in intentions to bring your subconscious mind up to speed with the programs you'd like it to be running, and releasing the ones you'd like to let go of.

Step One: Learn how to reach the Theta state & practice it. (See Chapter Six or the digital bonus material for ways to do this)

Step Two: Following the guidance of my Making Wishes video, make a list of things you want to invite, release or change. (Located in digital bonus material)

Step Three: Using my Program Writing video, change your wishes into programs that will go into your subconscious properly, as well as communicate your desires to the Universe. (Located in digital bonus material)

Step Four: Optional: Check into resources such as *Theta Healing, Diseases and Disorders* by Vienna Stibal, *You Can Heal Your Life* by Louise Hay to add to your programs or send your digital list to me at AphroditeBeaming@gmail.com and book a paid session for me to help add more valuable programs to your list if desired. I'd be more than happy to work with you on any of this.

Step Five: Record your list into an mp3 format sound recording. I usually record this in my voice for people who purchase the program, but your voice is tuned to the perfect frequency to heal you- so your own voice would be even more powerful than mine for this purpose. I'm not great tech support on this, so I suggest doing an Internet search on how to make a recording on your device if you don't know how- or ask a tech savvy friend to show you the ropes.

Here's the process for recording your own programs:

- Go into the Theta state with the intention for it to be infused into the recording. This creates a level of self-hypnosis.

- Ground, raise your vibration and start blasting Essence Healing energy with the intention it be infused into the recording.

- Press record.

- Continue keeping yourself in Theta & energy healing mode throughout the recording.

- Open with the following programs in a calm voice:

- I command that I be programmed with the following programs on every level, layer and aspect of my being for my highest good.

- I fully believe that transformation and healing in every respect is completely possible through the power of words, energy, intention and the mind.

- These programs work for me, whether I or anyone else, believe they will or not.

- Read your list of programs occasionally pausing in your reading to envision the programs implanting into your being.

- Close the recording with the following programs:

- I am now to be shown what each of these programs feels like, and they are activated within me and within my life

188

immediately with grace and ease.

- I command that my vibrational frequency be raised to match that of my higher self and my desires in their manifested state.

- My transition into these new programs will occur with total grace and ease.

- I command that I be programmed, on all levels, with the belief that every single one of these programs is possible and currently in progress.

- I command that these programs continue to be programmed in, by my mind, and work on me automatically and continually for as long as it takes to have them truly and deeply ingrained within my being, creating permanent positive change for the highest good of all.

- I command that any and all programs that contradict or block any of these new beneficial programs be dissolved released and replaced on every level, layer and aspect of my being now and forever.

- I command that these programs go out into the universe as a request to the divine, to fulfill these programs for my highest and best good. AND SO IT IS.

Note: It is up to you whether you follow this script, written in the "I am" format, or the way the video will tell you to do, which is putting it in the "you are" format. When you are recording for yourself, either way will work. If you choose to have me record for you, it will need to be in the "You are" format.

- Stop Recording.

Step Six: Listen to your recording every night for 30 nights minimum, as you're falling asleep.

Step Seven: Watch your life change & journal about it. Come up with more programs and make another recording each month until you feel well balanced and happy.

Note: You will also find a list of programs that are commonly used, as well as some worksheets to go with the videos in the digital materials link at the end of the book. The appropriate PDFs are included in the bonus material as well.

Here is the information I send along to people who purchase this program as to what to expect:

I recommend that you download the tracks, create 2 or 3 playlists and organize them this way:

Playlist 1:

- Evening Meditation (included in bonus material)
- Programs

Playlist 2:

- Daytime Meditation (included in bonus material)
- Programs

Playlist 3:

- Daytime Meditation (included in bonus material)

Listen to Playlist 1 every night with headphones as you drift off to sleep. Yes it is fine, and even preferred that you fall asleep while listening. You may wake up later and remove your headphones etc.

Listen at whatever volume is most comfortable for you. It is believed that even at a barely audible level, your brain is still picking up the vibration/meaning of the words.

I suggest you listen to this for a minimum of 30 nights in a row. If you fall asleep without listening for one night, it won't ruin everything- just listen again the first chance you get and stick with it as long as you can.

I've had a few people who listen to the programs, without the introductory meditations, on a very low volume in the background as they go about their daily activities. These people have had the most extraordinary results. Listening both as you sleep as well as randomly throughout the day seems to really set things in stone. Just make sure you're not allowing yourself to contradict the programs by mentally arguing or dismissing them. Whenever you tune into them, just think "yes please."

Playlists 2 & 3 are based on your personal preference. It

is generally recommended that people meditate daily- these recordings will give you that opportunity. Use them whenever you get the chance, choosing Playlist 2 if you'd like to use that time to deepen your programming, or Playlist 3 if you'd like to just use it to get in the zone or program in new things you've come up with by listing them silently while in the Theta state.

WHAT TO EXPECT

Some things in your life and your mind may begin changing and shifting immediately. Other times you may have a thought or epiphany, out of nowhere, that shows you how to achieve your intentions. You may occasionally feel a dull headache within your brain as your mind rewires itself into your new and improved state. Please see a doctor if your headaches are severe. The headache I'm talking about is extremely mild.

Know that it takes up to a year to completely rewire your brain into new habits, patterns, and beliefs. Old beliefs and struggles can come up during this process as with any transition. Know that they are coming up to be acknowledged and released - NOT for getting wrapped up in all over again. Just ride the wave as best you can, and acknowledge that you are going through a major shift.

If you notice the opposite of your intentions occurring, don't worry or resist. You can choose your actions on a conscious level, by recognizing that your subconscious mind is doing a lot of changing through this process. If certain programs have been running since you were very young, it may take some time for those programs to fully transition into the newly programmed beliefs and behaviors. The more you surrender/flow with it, the easier the transition will be.

I hope that you enjoy this journey into manifesting your desires. If you would like more information on The Law of Attraction, check out Abraham Hicks' vast collection of resources online. The top steps are: decide what you desire and focus on what you do want, rather than what you don't want. Focus on each desire for at least 90 seconds, feeling as though you have it already. Get these desires implanted into your subconscious mind, along with the belief that you can have them & match your frequency to what you want. This Metamorphosis system will assist you with all of that and more. Try it- what have you got to lose?

Chapter Thirteen

Professionalism

After 20 years in the spa industry, I've had a vast amount of training on professionalism and presentation. If you decide to do energy work professionally, I'm here to tell you that the way you present yourself and your space makes all the difference. You can bring through the most amazing energy and information, but if you have poor hygiene or dress sloppily, the majority of people will not return.

As much as we'd like to believe that appearances don't matter, the fact of the matter is that they do. Look at the messages people are inundated with every day through the media. This is what you're up against. I believe this may change as The Shift progresses, but for now it is something to consider. My suggestion is to visit local spas, salons, boutiques and healing centers to get some ideas on how to set up your space and how you might dress in order to make a good impression. Look at what impresses you and what doesn't. This will help you decide the best way to present yourself.

You don't necessarily have to go all out, but every day you should take a look at yourself and your surroundings and ask if this is how you want to present yourself. Think about yourself and your office as though you were a stranger looking at these things. What impression do you get? It may be common sense, but here are some things to consider when you decide to work with the public:

- Smelling like smoke, body odor or bad breath will turn most clients off.

- Wearing sloppy jeans, baggy clothes and t-shirts doesn't give off an air of professionalism. There is a difference between stylish jeans and casual wear. Pay attention to the distinction.

- Pets and pet hair can turn many people off- both in your healing space and on your clothing. Consider this when setting up your business and dressing for work. Warn your clients in advance if animals are regularly in your treatment room.

- Looking your best conveys confidence and attracts

more people to you.

- Your personal sense of style often reveals the type of person you are to others and allows them to decide whether you're someone they'd like to get to know or not.

- Be on time. Arriving 20-30 minutes before your first appointment will give you time to settle in, take care of any last minute things that pop up, and have you ready incase they arrive early. It does not look professional to be arriving at the same time as them, especially if it's on a regular basis.

- Building your internal confidence will help people perceive you as trustworthy on a subconscious level. See earlier chapters and book recommendations for inspiration.

- Decide how much of your personal life you will share with your clients. In the healing industry, boundaries are often thin. It is a good idea to trust your intuition on whom you share personal information with. In most industries, it is a good policy to keep your private life private, but in healing and intuitive work, we tend to attract people who mirror us. So pulling from our own life lessons often helps to guide them. Where you will draw the line is up to you. In a spa the rule is no talking about politics, sex or religion. However, healing work is often spiritual, and sex is a sacred practice- so politics may still be off the table, but to a certain extent the other topics are to be touched on carefully and professionally- customized to fit the comfort level of you and your client. Just remember to set the intention of making people comfortable and keeping the session focused more on them than on you.

- Does your workspace represent the quality of service you want to provide?

- Will people feel relaxed and comfortable in your space and around you?

- Go out into the community or online and look at people you'd like to emulate the careers of. How do they present themselves?

- Be polite.

- Smile and convey warmth.

- Don't gossip.

- Don't put down other lightworkers (healers, psychics...).

- Ask them if they'd like to book their next session before leaving.

- Business permits, liability waivers and insurance are a good idea for obvious reasons. (Google "liability insurance reiki" and "waivers reiki.") They are sometimes legally required by the state.

- Try to make everything as appealing as possible. Pay attention to the energy you and your space convey, as well as the appearance, smell, sounds and so on.

It doesn't necessarily cost a lot of money to begin presenting yourself and your business more professionally. Sometimes ironing your clothes or freshly painting a room can make the difference. Start simple and build as you can. If you struggle with these things, ask a stylish friend to help you out.

I know this seems like the least self-actualized section of this book. After empowering you to let go of people-pleasing habits and tendencies, I'm sure this seems like a suggestion to revert to unhealthy behaviors. It is not my intention to suggest that you be anything other than yourself. In fact, your clients will feel drawn to you when you're being real. It would just be in your best interest to make a good first impression so that people want to get to know you and will be more open to receiving what you can offer them. Think about it this way: if you were choosing a hairstylist you'd want one with a similar sense of style to yours, or an even better sense of style. When a client looks for a healer/psychic/coach, they want someone they feel has their act together. They want someone who exudes confidence, health and wisdom at the very least.

I don't want you to feel as though you need to wait until you're fully healed yourself before you begin working on others. Working on others is often part of our journey into self-healing. It is not a requirement that you be perfect or totally enlightened in order to do any of this work. However, you do want to make sure that you are capable of dealing with your clients, their issues and their possible reactions to your sessions. You should be well-balanced mentally. You should also only do this as a profession if you feel a deep calling to it. If it isn't beckoning to you as your purpose for being alive right now, don't do it. It's not easy to make a living doing this work unless you are fully driven to do it, and even then it can be as challenging as it is rewarding.

It is very important that you don't sit around and wait for people to come knocking on your door. Don't announce on Facebook that you're open for business and expect the world to sign up for your services. You have to prove you're good. You have to network, do events, go door to door at local businesses introducing yourself, get your name out there to as many people as possible, you may even pay a business coach to get you going. Try to find ways to do this that feel good to you, even if they're a little challenging or scary. It can't hurt to envision your practice full and thriving, but that alone won't bring the people. The epiphanies and inspirations that come after you meditate on your desires are what you need to pay attention to. Now go be awesome at whatever it is that you love.

Story Waters, Channeler

Lee Harris, Channeler

Lisa Gawlas, Channeler

Bonus Digital Materials

Go to www.AprilAdamsAuthor.com to sign up for the included digital bonus materials.

You will receive a link to a Dropbox folder entitled Essence Healing Book.

There you will find the following:

Activation Meditations, a series of meditation MP3s you can listen to in order to activate your healing abilities. These were recorded during an actual Essence Certification Class. They are numbered in order.

Chapter Twelve is a folder that contains everything you need to do the self-hypnosis process described in Chapter Twelve. This is also where you will find the link for Theta/Presence.

Resonance Programs is an MP3 recording you can listen to at night as you sleep in order to begin resonating with your Essence as well as your desires.

Special thanks to those I've loved in this lifetime and any other.

To my wife for inspiring me to begin this journey and loving me so intensely, even when I was broken. Oh and for helping me with the technical aspects of this book. I love you.

To my clients, whom I also consider my friends, for being my test subjects and inspiration for this knowledge.

To our culture for giving me stuff to work on so that I could help others and fulfill my purpose.

To my family: for the issues, the love and the support.

To Annette Meisel who has inspired me, even from the Great Beyond, to follow my own path.

To Laura Ezekiel for letting me know what I was capable of, and not letting me get away with playing it small.

To David M. Kane for all of the marketing help, kinship and assistance with the title. You are the Key.

To YOU, my fellow seeker.

To all of the metaphysical authors and channels who came before me.

And most of all…big gratitude to my own Essence, the Universe and the Divine. Wheeeeeee!!! What a ride.

April Adams owns The Retreat on Elm in Manchester, New Hampshire, where she works as an intuitive life coach, certified Presence meditation trainer, and Reiki Master. The creator of the Metamorphosis Hypnosis Program and the Essence Healing System, she has dedicated her life to helping people find fulfillment.

Having assisted countless women, and a few open-minded men, through their personal struggles by bringing passion, empowerment, and contentment to their lives, April specializes in combining the power of the mind with the power of the spirit to create the best possible life.

In her spare time April likes to read, dance and play in waterfalls with her wife and son.

AprilAdamsAuthor.com
FillingYourCup.com
AphroditeBeaming@gmail.com

Made in the USA
Middletown, DE
23 January 2015